SPIT AND PASSION

BLINDSPOT GRAPHICS

SPIT AND PASSION

WRITTEN AND ILLUSTRATED BY
CRISTY C. ROAD

THE FEMINIST PRESS
AT THE CITY UNIVERSITY OF NEW YORK
FEMINISTPRESS.ORG

TO FEELING NO SHAME IN FEAR,
NO DOUBT IN SURVIVAL,
AND NO SILENCE IN ANGER.

CHAPTER ONE

SHE SCREAMS IN SILENCE

WHEN THAT "MOVE THIS" CASSETTE SINGLE APPEARED ON MY KITCHEN TABLE, I COULD HAVE DIED. IT BECAME THE SOUNDTRACK TO MY FORBIDDEN GENES -- THE SACRILEGIOUS ONES THAT RAN LOOSE BENEATH MY KID-LIKE EXTERIOR. THE ORGANIC GENES. *THE REPRESSED GENES.*

"MOVE THIS" BY TECHNOTRONIC TOOK MY HAND AND LED ME TO A PROMISED LAND. AS DID "LA ISLA BONITA" AND "VOGUE" BY MADONNA, AND "MOVIENDO LAS CADERAS" BY ORO SOLIDO. THESE SONGS WERE VERBALLY DARING AND SYNONYMOUS WITH THE SPICE OF MY LIFE: SEXUALITY. WHAT WAS THIS? AND WHY DOES DANCE POP AND MERENGUE PENETRATE THE FIBERS OF MY NERVES, MY FINGERS, AND MY EYEBALLS? MY EYEBALLS STARED AT THE WOMEN DANCING, WONDERING IF I HAD TO BE THEM, IN ORDER TO MAYBE DATE THEM.

I KEPT MY IDENTITY TO MYSELF AS SOON AS I FOUND IT. I HAD SEEN IT BEFORE, IN CARTOON CHARACTERS: ANDROGYNOUS, SOFT SPOKEN CARTOON CHARACTERS LIKE BIG BIRD AND THE BRAVE LITTLE TOASTER. THEY DIDN'T HAVE TO BE A YOUNG GIRL OR A YOUNG BOY WITH DARK INSECURITIES AND STIGMATIZED DAYDREAMS. THEY COULD TRANSCEND AMBIGUOUSLY BETWEEN BOY, GIRL, HERO, VILLAIN, MARTYR.

I KEPT EVERYTHING TO MYSELF, INCLUDING MY RELATIONSHIP TO MEREN-GUE AND DANCE POP. IT WAS WHAT I LISTENED TO WHEN I IMAGINED LOVE — CONFLICTED, UNCOMPROMISING, ADULT LOVE. WHEN I IMAGINED YOUTH, HOPE, AND BUILDING THE BRIDGE TO MYSELF, I LISTENED TO AERSOMITH.

I FEARED WHAT MY FAMILY WOULD THINK, BUT I TRIED TO STAY CALM. I TRIED TO PRETEND EVERYONE ON EARTH WAS GAY. I TRIED TO PRETEND THE RELIGIOUS ICONS THROUGHOUT THE HOUSE COULD HEAR ME, AND ACCEPT ME.

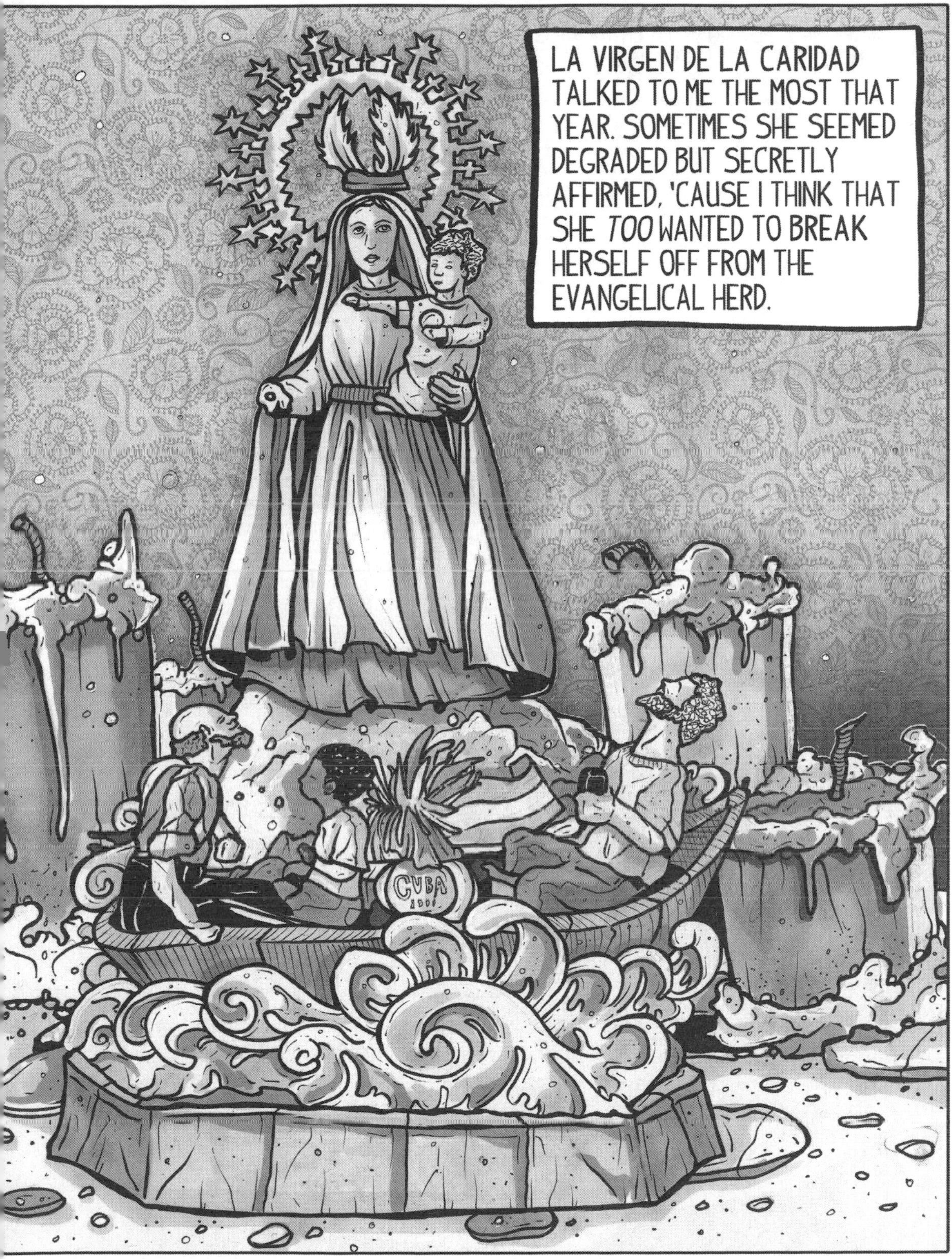
LA VIRGEN DE LA CARIDAD TALKED TO ME THE MOST THAT YEAR. SOMETIMES SHE SEEMED DEGRADED BUT SECRETLY AFFIRMED, 'CAUSE I THINK THAT SHE *TOO* WANTED TO BREAK HERSELF OFF FROM THE EVANGELICAL HERD.
CUBA

LA VIRGEN WAS THE MARTYR OUR ENTIRE VALUE SYSTEM WAS BASED UPON, SO WE LOOKED TO HER FOR BLESSINGS. OF ALL THE FIGURINES WHICH WHERE SCATTERED THROUGHOUT THE HOUSE — *LA VIRGEN* SPOKE THE MOST, THROUGH THE PERSPECTIVE OF A FEMALE MARTYR, AND NOT *JUST* THE MOTHER OF CHRIST.

AWARE OF THE POLITCAL ALLEGATIONS TIED TO CATHOLIC SYMBOLISM, I LIKED TO SEE IT ALL AS MY FAMILY'S ART AND FOLKLORE. LA VIRGEN WAS AN HEIRLOOM . . .

. . . RATHER THAN A PIONEER OF A SOCIAL REVOLUTION THAT SHACKLED MY ORGANS.

I, HOWEVER, WAS ON A QUEST TO FEEL THAT FOLKLORE SEARING THROUGH MY VEINS, AS I LISTENED TO MY HEART AND TO THE DEVIL'S MUSIC. I WAS ON A QUEST TO DEMYSTIFY THE NUTS AND BOLTS THAT TRANSFORMED THE CATHOLIC DOCTRINE INTO A NEEDLE, RATHER THAN A CELEBRATION.

THIS WAS A SPECIAL ERA, MANIFESTED THROUGH THE 15-MINUTE REVELATIONS BROUGHT TO US BY "VOGUE" BY MADONNA, CHARYTIN'S EXPOSED CLEAVAGE BEHIND HER SEQUINED TOPS, AND *REN & STIMPY*.

UNFORTUNATELY, THIS KNOWLEDGE HARDLY LEFT THE CONFINES OF MY ALLEGEDLY SICK HEAD.

DURING THIS ERA, THE DEFINITION OF SALVATION PLUNGED INTO A NEW ARMAGEDDON OF PRETEEN SELF-SUFFICIENCY. OR AT LEAST, AS MUCH SELF-SUFFICIENCY YOU COULD HAVE WHEN YOU'RE ELEVEN YEARS OLD, SHARING A ROOM WITH YOUR OLDER SISTER, WHO BEARS STRIKINGLY DIFFERENT TASTE THAN YOU, AND YOU ARE SORT OF IN THE CLOSET.

MY SISTER WAS NAMED ANGELINA, BUT WE ALL CALLED HER FIFI. FIFI AND I DIDN'T TALK ABOUT SEX AND IDENTITY POLITICS, BUT SHE SHARED MY FOND DISLIKE FOR THE WORLD AS IT WAS. TOGETHER, WE COULD HATE POPULAR CULTURE AND BE GREAT FRIENDS. SHE WAS QUICK AND WISE, AND I WAS ANGRY BUT ALIVE ON THE SURFACE. SHE IS A CAPRICORN AND I AM A GEMINI. SHE HELPED ME WORRY LESS BY SEEMING SO SURE OF HERSELF ALL THE TIME.

I LIVED WITH MY MAMA, THE PISCEAN MATRIARCH OF THE HOUSEHOLD WHO ALWAYS KEPT THE PEACE AND LED US THROUGH LIFE; MY GRANDMA YEYA, A SAGITTARIUS WITH SUCH UNCOMPROMISING SASS I'M CERTAIN SHE MUST HAVE HAD SOME FIERY ASPECT IN HER CHART; FIFI MY SISTER; TIA HORTENCIA, A LIBRA HIGH SCHOOL TEACHER; AND PRINCESS PENNY, OUR CHIHUAHUA, WHO WAS YEYA'S BIGGEST ADMIRER.

NEXT DOOR WAS TIA ESPERANZA, ANOTHER SAGITTARIUS WHOM I COULD TRUST WITH MY DEEPEST SECRET CELEBRITY CRUSHES ON SENSITIVE GUYS LIKE RON PALLILO AND BOB COSTAS. WITH HER LIVED MY TWO COUSINS: SANTIAGO (SAGITTARIUS) AND LITTLE GABRIEL (VIRGO).

GIVEN OUR ASTROLOGICAL MAKE-UP, I WAS CLEARLY THE ONE IN THE FAMILY WITH ALL THE UNCERTAIN FEELINGS. IDENTITY WAS PRECIOUS AND SCARY. COMMUNICATING ITS POTENCY IN THE MOST TENDER MANNER POSSIBLE HAD BECOME MY LIFE'S WORK. DESPITE THE UNCHARTED DEPTHS MY BRAIN WAS TUMBLING INTO, AND DESPITE THE TRADITIONS OF *LA FAMILIA CUBANA*, THERE WAS LOVE IN MY FAMILY, WHETHER WE BICKERED, SULKED, OR ESCAPED.

I LOOKED FORWARD TO BEING OLD AND DONE WITH THE WHOLE "FINDING MYSELF" SPIEL, BUT FOR THE TIME BEING, I WAS OKAY HIDING IN MY PASTEL-PINK CONCRETE SQUARE WHERE MY FOUR LOVING CUBANAS WERE ALWAYS CALLING ON MY ATTENTION AND OFFERING ME FOOD EVERY SO OFTEN.

HOME FELT SAFE ENOUGH TO NOT HAVE TO BE ANYONE I DID NOT WANT TO BE, AS LONG AS I DIDN'T TALK ABOUT THE THINGS I WAS USUALLY THINKING ABOUT.

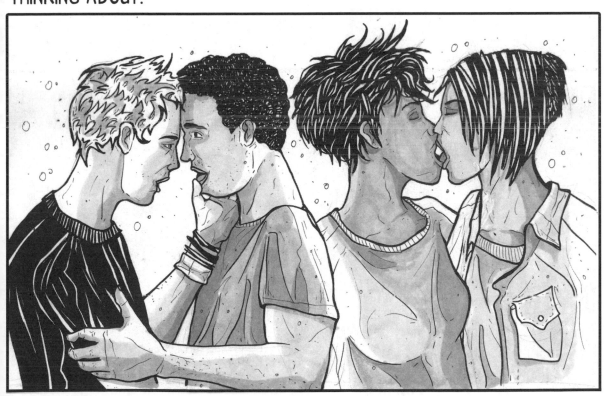

MY HOME LIFE CONSISTED OF A FORBIDDEN EXPLORATION OF THE POLITICS OF DESIRE. I WOULD WADDLE INTO THE BATHROOM SEVERAL TIMES A DAY, LOCKING THE DOOR, CHASING AFTER THE LIVELIEST BENEDICTION OF MY FUNCTIONALITY. I DIDN'T EVEN KNOW THAT JERKING OFF WAS AN ACTUAL THING PEOPLE TALKED ABOUT UNTIL I HEARD ABOUT IT ON *ROSEANNE*. THE MECHANICS WERE UNFATHOMABLE TO ME, ESPECIALLY THE WHOLE "ORGASM" PORTION THAT I HEARD WAS SUPPOSED TO MOVE MOUNTAINS.

ON A SPRING DAY IN 1993, JERKING OFF FELT DIFFER-ENT, LIKE A SLIDE INTO A PORTAL OF SEMI-ADULTHOOD WHERE I COULD DEFINE SEXUALITY ON MY OWN TWO FEET, WITH MY OWN TWO HANDS. THERE WAS LESS MENTAL DIVERSION AS MY THOUGHTS SETTLED IN AN UNUSUAL PLATEAU. IN IT, I FOUND MORE PLEASURE AND LESS SIN, LESS OF A QUEST FOR KNOWLEDGE AND MORE OF AN IGNITION.

AS SOME GIRL DANCED AROUND ON A COP SHOW, I FELL FACE FIRST INTO AN UNPARALLELED STATE OF EUPHORIA.

MY BRAIN TUGGED AT THE BACK OF MY EYEBALLS; MY ANKLES FROZE AND I WANTED TO SCREAM AND CRAWL, OR OTHERWISE EXPLODE.

AND AS THE AFTERNOON SUN SET BEHIND ME,

I HAD AN ORGASM FOR THE FIRST TIME.

(EXCEPT I ACTUALLY HAD NO CLUE AS TO WHAT HAD JUST HAPPENED.)

THE SENSATION WAS COMFORTING, BUT FRIGHTENING WHEN PAIRED WITH THE REST OF REALITY. YOU HEAR OVER AND OVER FROM THE CHRISTIAN RIGHT THE NOTION THAT "MASTURBATION" IS AN "INFESTATION" BECAUSE

YOU DON'T KNOW WHERE THOSE HANDS HAVE BEEN.

BUT WAS THAT JESUS AND THE APOSTLES? OR THEIR PRESENT-DAY CONSPIRATORS? I HAD LITTLE EDUCATION ON THIS, SO FOR A SECOND I WONDERED IF I HAD IMPREGNATED MYSELF.

I WONDERED IF SEXUAL LIBERATION WAS ACTUALLY *UNHEALTHY*, OR DID THEY JUST WANT US TO *THINK* THAT?

BECAUSE RIGHT THEN AND THERE — I FELT ALIVE.

I LIVED INSIDE MY HEAD, ON AN ISOLATED MEMBRANE, CONCERNED WITH REALITY BUT AFRAID OF THE ANSWERS.

MY FAMILY WAS A TRADITIONAL CUBAN CONCOCTION OF UNBRIDLED LOVE AND PROTECTION. THEY CARED FOR MY WELL-BEING AND SHOWED ME HOW IMPORTANT I WAS.

MY FAMILY ALSO PROTECTED ME FROM HYPERSEXUALIZED AMERICAN CULTURE, GAY THEMES ON TELEVISION, AND SLUMBER PARTIES — UNTIL I TURNED 18, OF COURSE.

FOR THE TIME BEING, I DIDN'T REALLY MIND MUCH. I COULD STAY HERE WITH MR. HORSE, CUBAN FOOD, TV DINNERS, AND THESE KID-CENTERED ROLE MODELS THAT SCREAMED **GAY! FARTS! BOOGERS! TOMBOYHOOD!** AND **DIRT!** AT THE END OF THE DAY, MY FAMILY DID NOT SEEM TO SEE HOW GAY *REN 3 STIMPY* TRULY WERE.

IT WAS FINALLY THE LAST SEMESTER OF GRADE SCHOOL.

I MANEUVERED THROUGH BODIES THAT WEREN'T TAUNTED, AND I FELT RELATIVELY ALONE, AS EVERY GIRL IN MY FIFTH GRADE CLASS HAD A LITTLE BOYFRIEND TO SEND NOTES TO. WE WERE ELEVEN YEARS OLD, DRY OF ANY EXPLANATIONS OF WHY THE WORLD WAS THE WAY IT WAS, AND WHY "SAD AND THOUGHT PROVOKING" WAS SCARY — WHILE "PERKY AND VIVACIOUS" WAS ALIVE.

FIFTH GRADE HAD BEEN A DARK TUNNEL OF CHANCE ENCOUNTERS WITH LITTLE PEOPLE WHO I WISHED WOULD BE MY FRIENDS, OR I WISHED WOULD JUST GO AWAY.

SOMEWHERE FAR, FAR AWAY.

I FELT PROUD OF MY CONVICTIONS, BUT MY OUTSIDES WERE TORMENTED, AND IF ANOTHER 11-YEAR-OLD BOY EVER MADE FUN OF MY UNIBROW OR MY SIDEBURNS AGAIN, I SWORE TO MYSELF I WOULD CUT HIM. AND THEN THERE WAS NATALIA. NATALIA FELT BETTER THAN EVERYONE BECAUSE HER FATHER HAD PROPERTY IN BAL HARBOUR. BECAUSE "GOD LOVES CUBANS." SO I WONDERED IF GOD LOVED ALL CUBANS, AND JUST SOME MORE THAN OTHERS? OR IF PEOPLE ONLY PROSPERED WHEN GOD LOVED THEM? OR IF GOD ONLY LOVED RICH PEOPLE? MAYBE GOD WOULD LOVE MY FAMILY MORE AND MAKE US RICH LIKE NATALIA IF I STOPPED HAVING ORGASMS? OR MAYBE GOD LOVED EVERYONE, AND RICH PEOPLE JUST THOUGHT GOD LOVED THEM MORE BECAUSE THEY PUT #20 BILLS IN THE DONATION BASKET WHEN IT'S PASSED AROUND AT WEDDINGS?

I NEVER CUT ANYONE.

ADOLESCENCE WAS TOO FRIGHTENING, TOO
UNCHARTED. SO FAR, I LEARNED ROCK MUSICIANS
WERE MOST LIKELY OUTRAGEOUS DRUG ADDICTS, GAY
PEOPLE WERE UNCOUTH AND NOT FOR CHILDREN'S
VIRGIN EYES, AND MASTURBATION WAS AN ACT OF
FILTH. I LEARNED CHUBBY SHORT GIRLS WITH HAIRY
FACES LIKE ME COULDN'T RUN FAST AND MAY NEVER
KISS ANYONE ON THE MOUTH. I LEARNED THAT HUMAN
BEINGS SHOULD NOT BE GAY IF THEY WANTED TO
SURVIVE A DAY ON THIS EARTH, CONVENTIONALLY,
WITH EASE. I LEARNED I WAS WALKING ON THIN ICE IF I
CONTINUED TO DEVELOP INTO THE ANGRY, YOUNG
PRODUCT OF THE IDENTITY I WAS BORN INTO.

SO? I FEEL SAD SOMETIMES ... AND DECONSTRUCTING THE FABRIC OF MY CARDBOARD BOX AND THE ANTI-BODIES WHICH SURROUNDED IT FELT MORE FUN THAN A BULLSHIT SLUMBER PARTY ANYWAY.

WHO NEEDED LOVE AND GOSSIP WITH STRAIGHT 11-YEAR-OLDS IN ORDER TO EXIST WHEN BODILY PLEASURE WAS ACCESSIBLE, WITHOUT THE VAST DIATRIBE THAT WAS TALKING TO PEOPLE — OR ABOUT PEOPLE — WHO I MIGHT WANT TO KISS ON THE LIPS? AT SLUMBER PARTIES, ALL THE GIRLS WERE PROBABLY JUST GOING TO SIT AROUND AND RAVE ABOUT JASON PRIESTLY, SIGNALING THE CROSS WHILE SECRETLY GETTING WET FROM THE THOUGHT OF HIM. GOD.

AT LEAST STOP MAKING ME FEEL LIKE THE ONLY FREAK WHO JERKS OFF, FOR CRYING OUT LOUD.

I PERSONALLY THOUGHT JASON PRIESTLY LOOKED LIKE BULLSHIT. I LIKED THE MADE UP PEOPLE IN MY THOUGHTS, PRANCING AROUND ME WITH LONG, RATTED HAIR, BIG ASSES IN THE WAY OF EVERYTHING, EMPOWERED BREASTS IN VARYING SHAPES OF ANYTHING, AND AGGRESSION. ALL MY THOUGHTS WERE BASED ON THE OCCASIONAL GLIMPSES I GOT OF ADULT BODY PARTS IN WOMEN'S SPORTS.

SO, I DIDN'T HAVE ANYBODY TO EXPLAIN THE UNFATH-OMABLE, UNFORGIVING WARMTH OF AN ORGASM AT 7A.M., BECAUSE OF SOME GUY NAMED JESUS CHRIST, OR RATHER, THE GOVERNMENTS THAT TAINTED HIS HUMANITY. I FORGET THAT'S JUST THE SYSTEM WE ARE BORN INTO, AND WE EITHER LIKE IT, OR WE DON'T.

I DID NOT.

A DIFFERENT SORT OF ISOLATION SHAPED ITSELF BENEATH MY FEET AND INSIDE OF ME. ISOLATION PAIRED WITH ECSTASY, AND A SMEAR OF WOMANHOOD.

CHRIST'S POLITICAL AGENDA

I HAD COALESCED WITH THE OTHER KIDS IN MY FAMILY FOR MOST OF MY LIFE, DESPITE UNINVITED TRANSFORMATIONS. WE SWUNG BACK AND FORTH BETWEEN DRESSING DOLLS AND BUILDING ROBOTICS. FROM SANTIAGO AND ME BUILDING DEATH TRAPS FOR THE NEW KIDS ON THE BLOCK, TO THE TELEVISION STATION FIFI AND I INVENTED, WHICH SHOWCASED OUR FAVORITE ANTI-TEEN-CULTURE ICONS SUCH AS JERRY ORBACH AND SALLY STRUTHERS — WE WERE OUTSIDERS TOGETHER. MY SISTER, COUSINS, AND I WERE TUMBLING DOWN THE ROAD BESIDE THEIR MOTHER, HER SISTER, MY MOTHER, HER MOTHER, AND THE LITTLE BIRDS AND DOGS THAT REMINDED US HOW MUCH ART, IRRELEVANCE, AND COMMOTION MADE US HAPPY.

ASIDE FROM MY COUSINS, I HAD A FALTERING CONNECTION WITH THE MEN IN MY FAMILY. THEY WERE EITHER DISTANT, LOST, OR ROTTEN. EXCEPT MY ABUELITO, WHO PASSED AWAY WHEN I WAS ABOUT 3 YEARS OLD. ABUELITO WAS A LOVING MAN AND A FASHION ICON WITH SLICKED BACK GRAY HAIR AND A FRESHLY IRONED GUAYABERA. BUT AT THE END OF THE DAY, I CRADLED THE FACT THAT I WAS RAISED BY A GANG OF **BOISTEROUS CUBAN WOMEN.**

AND NO, NOT *WOMYN WITH A "Y,"* BUT WOMEN WITH A "FUCK YOU—*WE ARE WORKING-CLASS LATINAS."*

I TOOK PRIDE IN RELATING TO THE TOUGH BOYS AT SCHOOL WITH HIDDEN STASHES OF PORNOGRAPHY, AND THE SENSITIVE BOYS WITH HIDDEN AGENDAS, BUT I DID NOT KNOW WHERE TO GO FROM THERE. MY DEEP CONNECTION TO MALES IN GENERAL WAS EVER CHANGING; SO I ALWAYS FELT LIKE I WAS SOMEWHERE IN THE MIDDLE OF MEN AND WOMEN. MY CONNECTION AND OBSESSION WITH MEN WAS NOT ROMANTIC, BUT CURIOUS AND COMPETITIVE (UNLESS, OF COURSE, IF IT WAS TOWARD A SENSITIVE NEWS ANCHOR LIKE BOB COSTAS). MY INTROSPECTIVE NATURE WAS BASED ON FEAR . . . AND I WONDERED IF ANYBODY WAS BEGINNING TO NOTICE THAT I WAS ACTUALLY GAY.

MAMA HAD A BOYFRIEND.

HIS NAME WAS MIGUEL AND HE WAS PRETTY COOL, UNLIKE WHAT YOU WOULD ASSUME OF YOUR MOTHER'S BOYFRIEND. I WAS GRATEFUL FOR THIS; CASUALLY SOCIALIZING WITH AN OLDER, STRAIGHT MAN WAS COMFORTING FOR THE FIRST TIME IN MY ENTIRE PRE-TEEN LIFE. MIGUEL WAS CUBAN, FROM NEW YORK CITY, AND HAD A RELATIVE UNDERSTANDING OF MY BOYISH NEEDS. I SOMETIMES HOPED AND WONDERED IF SOME OF HIS BEST FRIENDS IN JUNIOR HIGH WERE ANGRY TOMBOYS.

ALL WE NEED IS LOVE. IT'S TRUE. BUT THERE IS A MONSTER RUMBLING BENEATH THE SURFACE OF ANY CUBAN HOUSEHOLD WITH TRADITIONAL CATHOLIC VALUES.

CASUAL HOMOPHOBIA. IT'S THE SOCIAL ACCEPTANCE OF GAY JOKES, SLURS, AND HOMOPHOBIC REMARKS WHEN IN THE PRESENCE OF A FEMININE MAN OR A MASCULINE WOMAN. I SAW IT AS A SIDE EFFECT OF MONEY AND POWER DESTROYING SPIRITUALITY. FAMILY VALUES WERE NOW TAINTED WITH THE LEARNED CONCEPT OF HOMOPHOBIA.

CLOSED FOR RENOVATIONS

BECAUSE OF THIS, HOMOSEXUALITY (A POTENTIALLY COMMON IDENTITY TRAIT) WAS DOOMED, CLASSIFIED AS REBELLION LIKE ROCK'N'ROLL, GANGSTA RAP, AND SKIPPING CLASS. SO, I FOUND MY CLOSET, WITH THE TRUTH SEALED TIGHT.

MY LIFE AT HOME WAS THE ONLY SAFE MIDDLE GROUND I KNEW, WHERE I COULD BE CONFUSED WITHOUT HAVING TO CONSTANTLY JUSTIFY OR EXPLAIN IT.
EVERY SO OFTEN, I LEFT MY FAMILY WORRIED ABOUT THE DISCONNECT EXPOSED BY MY BLANK STARES AS EVERYONE ELSE LAUGHED AT THAT FUNNY THING SOMEONE HAD SAID ABOUT GAY PEOPLE.

I HAD MY SECRETS, BUT I LIKED TO PRETEND THAT THERE WASN'T MUCH TO HIDE. I LIKED TO PRETEND THAT THE CUFFS IN MY JEANS AND THE DIRT ON MY KNEES TOLD MY STORY. I LIKED TO PRETEND THE SINGLE BRAID THAT DRAPED ACROSS MY BACK GAVE THE ILLUSION OF A BUTCH HAIRCUT I MAY NEVER FEEL SAFE ENOUGH TO HAVE. MY COUSINS, MY SISTER, AND I WERE STILL BEST FRIENDS, BUT AS ADOLESCENCE BEGAN TO TAKE OVER, THE ISOLATION TRUNDLED BENEATH US AND HELD ME AT NIGHT. AS EVERYONE SLEPT, I HID IN A COCOON WITH MY BLOOD VESSELS AND MY INHIBITIONS.

CHAPTER TWO

WORDS I MIGHT HAVE ATE

SUMMER 1993

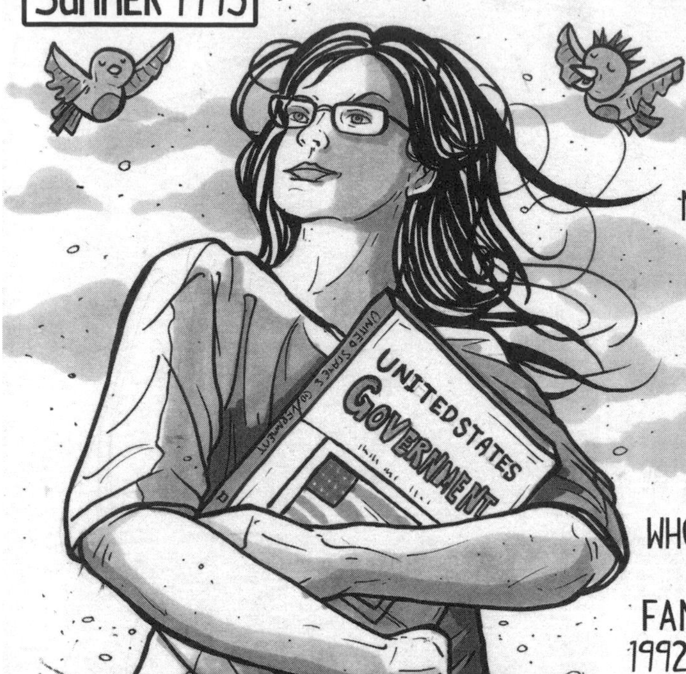
UNITED STATES
GOVERNMENT

MY INTEREST HAD DIVERTED FROM THE USUAL GAMES FIFI, SANTIAGO, GABRIEL AND I ENJOYED TOGETHER. NOW THAT IT WAS SUMMER AND I HADN'T REALLY MADE ANY FRIENDS, I MISSED TALKING TO STRANGERS IN CLASS. I STILL FELT A DEEP COMMONALITY WITH THE OTHER KIDS IN THE FAMILY AND WITH HORTENCIA. HORTY WAS MY LIBERAL-MINDED AUNT; A HIGH SCHOOL GOVERNMENT TEACHER WHO WAS A KID AT HEART. HORTY REPRESENTED THE TRAILBLAZING OF MY FAMILY'S POLITICAL VALUES. DURING THE 1992 ELECTIONS, WE WERE ASKED TO WRITE ABOUT OUR CHOICE FOR A PRESIDENTIAL CANDIDATE. AS MIAMI'S CUBAN POPULATION, AND THE ENTIRE STUDENT BODY OF JOSEPHINE SANTA CRUZ ELEMENTARY HAPPILY SUPPORTED

GEORGE BUSH SENIOR AND HIS ANTI-ABORTION POLICIES, HORTY PUSHED THE NOTION THAT BILL CLINTON CARED FOR WOMEN'S RIGHTS. SHE HELPED ME WRITE MY PAPER, ALLOWING ME TO BE THE ONLY STUDENT IN THE ENTIRE CLASSROOM WHO CHOSE CLINTON. PERHAPS SHE WAS ALSO TORTURED BY OUR LOCAL SOCIETY AND ITS INABILITY TO QUESTION TRADITION. PERHAPS MY SISTER AND COUSINS WERE ALSO AT A LOSS AS FAR AS WHERE TO GO FROM HERE AND WHAT TO BELIEVE IN. PERHAPS WE WERE ALL PERPLEXED, BUT UNABLE TO EXPRESS IT. TOGETHER, WE ENTERED THE DARK TUNNEL OF ADOLESCENCE THAT CHASTISED OUR ORGANS AND ACCENTUATED OUR FEAR OF GOD.

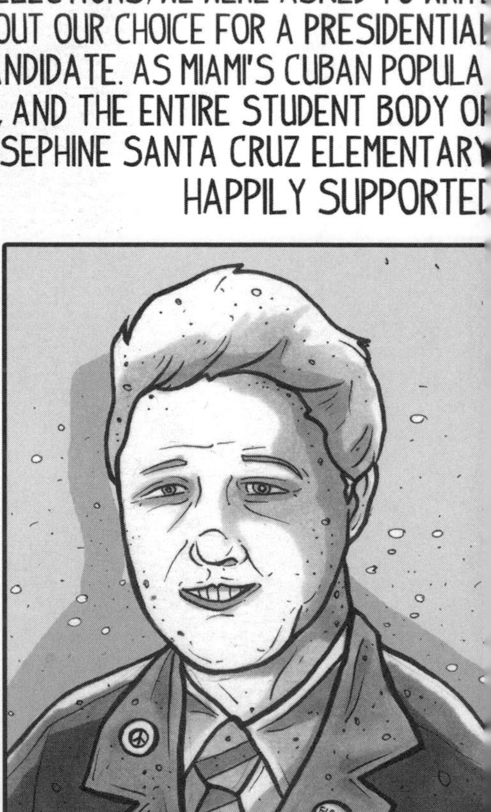
FLEET WOOD MAC

HAVING GROWN UP AROUND SALSA AND LATIN POP, I WANTED SOMETHING FOREIGN, BECAUSE FUCK, I FELT FOREIGN — LIKE AN ALIEN FROM GAY SPACE. I WANTED SOMETHING SLIGHTLY MORE TORTURED THAN MADONNA OR ORO SOLIDO, NO MATTER HOW MUCH I NEEDED TO VOGUE MYSELF TO SLEEP. THANK GOD I RECOGNIZED QUEEN FROM *WAYNE'S WORLD* WHEN I SAW THAT TAPE AT ESPERANZA'S. MY LOVE FOR MUSICALS BROUGHT ME AS CLOSE TO OUTCAST AS ANYTHING COULD. SOMETIMES I SAT BELOW A LIME TREE AND LISTENED TO QUEEN, PICKING AT THE THORNS WHEN THINKING BECAME TEDIOUS — TEARING APART A LIME WHEN PICKING BECAME COMPULSIVE.

MY LOVE FOR FREDDIE MERCURY GAVE ME WINGS . . .

. . . AND TOGETHER, WE EXISTED IN AN IMAGINARY VORTEX OF THE FUTURE.

I KNEW WHAT PUNK ROCK WAS. I WAS ACTUALLY **OBSESSED** WITH THE IDEA THAT THESE "PUNKS" TROLLED ABOUT THE PLANET QUESTIONING THE STATUS QUO. I SAW PUNKS ONCE — ON *ALVIN AND THE CHIPMUNKS*. I WAS FLOORED FOR 24 HOURS.

WHAT A LIFESTYLE.

I WAS ABOUT 4 YEARS OLD AND I SAW AN EPISODE CALLED "CHIP-PUNK," WHERE THE CHIPMUNKS PURSUE A PUNK ROCK IDENTITY AND END UP RUNNING FROM THE COPS AFTER PLAYING AN UNDERGROUND CLUB. AS THEY RAN, THEY DAYDREAMED OF WHAT JAIL WOULD FEEL LIKE. THE IMAGES DEEPLY AFFECTED ME, PARTLY BECAUSE IT HURT TO SEE THE CHIPMUNKS IN JAIL AND PARTLY BECAUSE SOMEWHERE THERE WAS MUSIC SO FROWNED UPON BY THE MAINSTREAM, BUT SO IMPOR-TANT, THE PUNKS WOULD RISK ARREST FOR THE SAKE OF PLAYING A SHOW.

I LIKED TO BELIEVE LA VIRGEN DE LA CARIDAD DIDN'T MIND MY INTEREST IN PUNK OR QUEEN, DESPITE HER FLOCK'S INTERPRETATION OF *THE DEVIL'S MUSIC*. RUNNING THE TIPS OF MY FINGERS THROUGH THE FOLDS IN HER GOWN, I WONDERED IF HER PERSUASION WAS REAL, AND THE CHRISTIAN-RIGHT-APPROPRIATED SAINTS AND APOSTLES WERE, IN FACT, RIGHT ABOUT THE FABRIC OF THE EARTH. PUTTING MY FINGER BETWEEN THE CREVICES, THE PASSENGERS OF THE SHIP AND ALONG THE SCULPTED WAVES, I TRIED TO PULL OUT THE ONE DISPLACED FIGURINE THAT I USED TO STEAL AND PLAY WITH. I REALIZED IT HAD BEEN GLUED DOWN. EVERYTHING WAS CHANGING. I DECIDED LA VIRGEN RECONSTRUCTED THE MEANING TO EVERYTHING, DISMANTLING THE TYPICAL DOCTRINES OF HER FOLLOWERS FOR THE SAKE OF MY OWN SALVATION. SHE WASN'T A TOY ANYMORE -- SHE WAS AN ARTISTIC TRADITION, AN IDEOLOGY THAT NEEDED WORK, AND A WOMAN WHO MIGHT HAVE HONORED OTHER WOMEN, BUT WE WILL NEVER KNOW, BECAUSE SO MUCH OF HER HISTORY HAS ALREADY BEEN **DESTROYED BY PATRIARCHY.**

SHE'S OFFICIALLY GAY. I *HOPE* YOU UNDERSTAND.

I STARTED THE SIXTH GRADE AT J.R. RIVERO MIDDLE SCHOOL IN SEPTEMBER 1993. THIS WAS, AFTER ALL, THE BEGINNING OF JUNIOR HIGH, *THE BEGINNING OF THE END OF CHILDHOOD.* SO I SPENT THE ENTIRE FIRST SEMESTER AND THE ENTIRE WINTER BREAK FIGURING OUT WHAT MY IDENTITY WAS GOING TO BE.

BOY, DID IT SUCK TO REALIZE I MAY HAVE BEEN WRONG ALL ALONG. THAT MY STAKE AT REBELLION WAS GUIDED BY COUNTER-REVOLUTIONARY IDEALS THAT MADE ME FEEL UGLIER BY THE SECOND. WHETHER MY SOUL BELONGED TO FREDDIE MERCURY, CLASSIC ROCK, OR HEAVY METAL, NONE OF IT ANSWERED MY PLEAS. I DIDN'T MIND THAT THE HEAVY METAL GIRLS WERE OVERSEXUALIZED, AS LONG AS THE MEN KEPT ON THEIR SPANDEX G-STRING/LEATHER PANT SETS ... I JUST WISHED THERE WERE **A RANGE OF WOMEN APPEARING IN VARIOUS PLACES**: PERFORMING IN BANDS, REPRESENTING AN ARRAY OF BODY TYPES AND HAIRCUTS; AND WHILE WE'RE AT IT, MAYBE SOME OUT MALE PERFORMERS? MAYBE SOME CAGE BOYS? MAYBE SOME GAY PEOPLE? **MAYBE IF JUDAS PRIEST WAS AS GAY AS THEY SEEMED TO BE?**

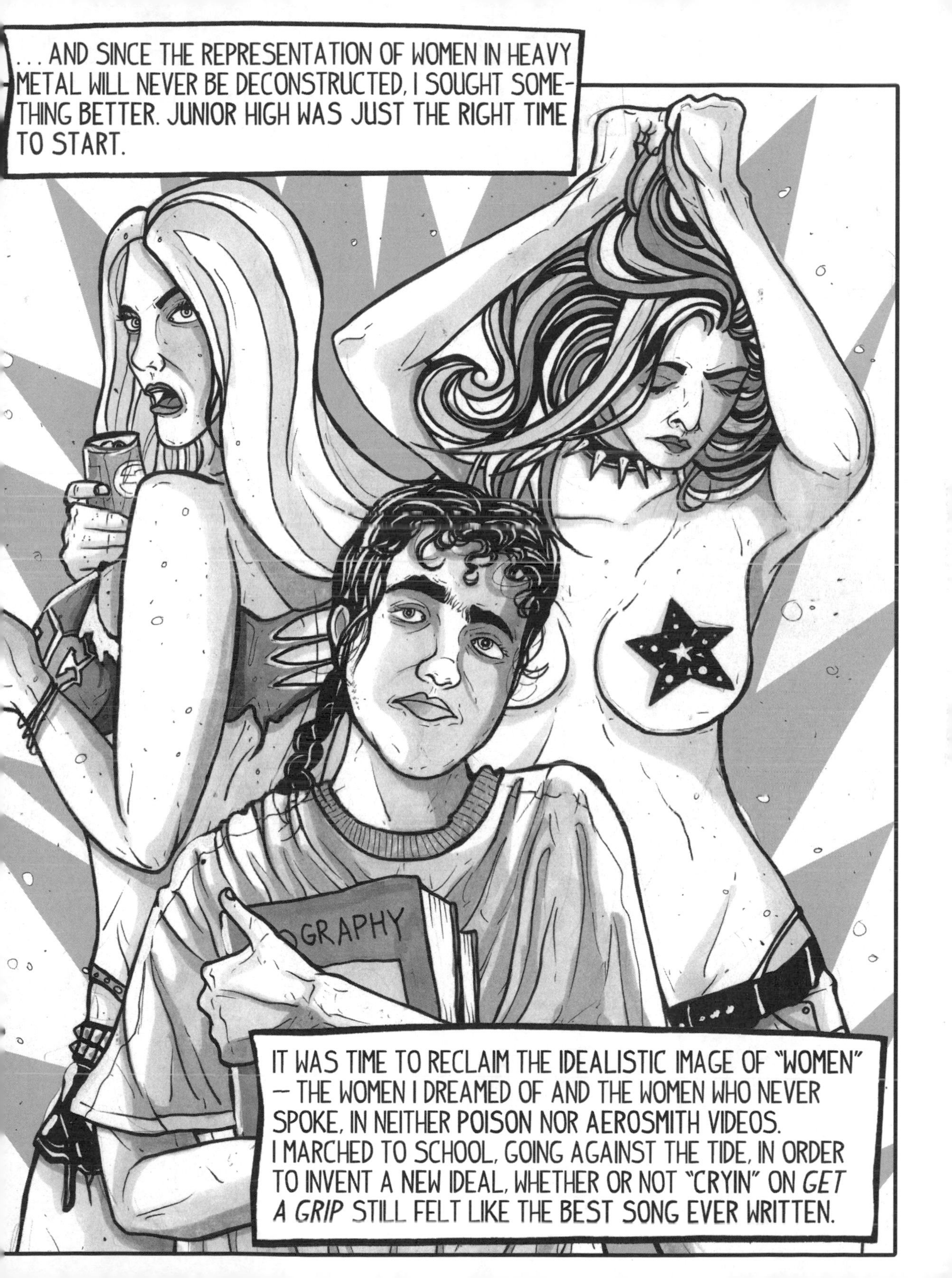
. . . AND SINCE THE REPRESENTATION OF WOMEN IN HEAVY METAL WILL NEVER BE DECONSTRUCTED, I SOUGHT SOMETHING BETTER. JUNIOR HIGH WAS JUST THE RIGHT TIME TO START.
GRAPHY
IT WAS TIME TO RECLAIM THE IDEALISTIC IMAGE OF "WOMEN" — THE WOMEN I DREAMED OF AND THE WOMEN WHO NEVER SPOKE, IN NEITHER POISON NOR AEROSMITH VIDEOS. I MARCHED TO SCHOOL, GOING AGAINST THE TIDE, IN ORDER TO INVENT A NEW IDEAL, WHETHER OR NOT "CRYIN" ON *GET A GRIP* STILL FELT LIKE THE BEST SONG EVER WRITTEN.

I FELT DRY OF ENLIGHTENMENT ON MY FIRST DAY OF THE SECOND SEMESTER OF THE SIXTH GRADE. I WAS, HOWEVER, EXHAUSTED FROM ALL OF THIS COMING-OUT-TO-MY-SOUL AND FINDING-AN-IDENTITY BUSINESS. I DIDN'T EXPECT THIS SEMESTER TO BE ANYTHING DIFFERENT. I EXPECTED FOR PEOPLE TO MAKE JOKES ABOUT MY LACK OF ATHLETIC ABILITY. I EXPECTED TO ONLY DO GOOD IN ART CLASS, AND TO OCCASIONALLY HATE MYSELF WHILE RUMMAGING ON AN ENDLESS TREK TO FIND A VOICE, OR AT LEAST SOME HOMOS.

CARLITO WAS THE FIRST PERSON I WAS REALLY FASCINATED BY IN JUNIOR HIGH. WE MET AT THE BACK OF SCIENCE CLASS. IT WAS THE FIRST TIME THE SUBJECT OF **HOMOSEXUALITY** EVER APPEARED, WITHOUT ME EVEN **TRYING.**

OUR TEACHER, MR. SUAREZ WAS GAY (MAKING IT CLEAR THROUGH THE MOST GENIUS OF EXPRESSIONS) AND ALTHOUGH EVERYONE LOVED HIS EASY GOING ATTITUDE TO-WARDS FORMAL EDUCATION . . .

I SAW HIM CHECKING YOU OUT, FRANKIE

SHUT UP FAGGOT !

HE LIKES YOU

YEAH I'M A *FAGIT* —A FEMALE ASS-GRABBER, INCLUDING TITS! HEH HEH HEH . . .

. . . THE INAPPROATE GAY SLURS (AND UNINTELIGIBLE ACRONYMS) STILL EXIT THE KIDS MOUTHS AT LUNCH, WHEN HE WASNT AROUND.

I HEARD RUMORS OF THE WORDS OF WISDOM MR. SUAREZ WOULD CASUALLY TOSS OUT IN HIS OTHER CLASSES, PARTICULARLY THE EIGHTH GRADE BIOLOGY CLASS. I BECAME MESMERIZED BY MR. SUAREZ . . .

. . . AND SUDDENLY I FELT MILDLY ENTHUSI- ASTIC ABOUT THIS PLACE. SCHOOL WAS UNFAIR, BUT IT WAS STILL THE OUTSIDE WORL . . . CARLITO SWORE I HAD A PROBLEM, SOME THING I WAS NOT TALKING ABOUT. SO HE TO ME I SHOULD LISTEN TO PUNK ROCK MUSIC.

AN *ORGASM* IS THE BEST FEELING YOU WILL **EVER** EXPERIENCE!

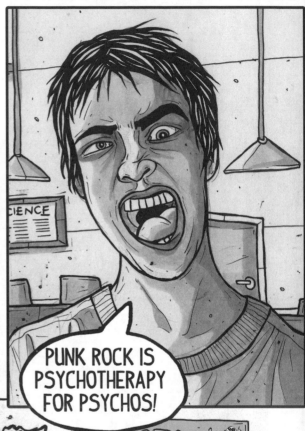

PUNK ROCK IS PSYCHOTHERAPY FOR PSYCHOS!

I BELIEVED I WAS PART PSYCHO, SO I ASKED HIM TO LEND ME A FEW TAPES. HE LENT ME *MY WAR* BY BLACK FLAG, *DOOKIE* BY GREEN DAY, AND *ROCK N ROLL NIGHTMARE* BY RICH KIDS ON LSD. I TOOK THEM, AND HOLDING THEM GAVE ME A NEW SENSE OF SECURITY. I RUBBED THE ARTWORK ON EACH COVER WITH MY INDEX FINGER, SMELLING THE FOLDS, LIKE IT WAS THE NIGHT BEFORE CHRISTMAS OR THE FIRST DAY OF SPRING. THE TOUCH RENEWED MY SENSES, AND I HELD THEM UNTIL SCHOOL WAS OVER THAT DAY.

I DIDN'T REALLY LIKE
BLACK FLAG OR
RICH KIDS ON LSD.
I FOUND BOTH OF THEM
BORING, AND NOTHING I
COULD REALLY FEEL
CONNECTED TO. BE-
CAUSE OF THIS, I WAS
EMBARRASSED BY
THE TRUTH THAT I ONLY
ENJOYED MUSIC THAT
RESEMBLED BROADWAY
MUSICALS, DISNEY
SOUNDTRACKS (LIKE
ALADDIN AND *THE LION
KING*), OR TELEVISION
THEME SONGS. I PUT
ON THE GREEN DAY CD
EXPECTING A SIMILAR
CALIBER OF BOREDOM.

INSTEAD, I WAS
TRANSFORMED. I FELT
PROTECTED AND
WARM -- ALIVE AND
IN LOVE.

I ENTERED THE WORLD OF *DOOKIE*, AND I FOUND MYSELF LYING UNDER A PILE OF DOG SHIT AND DIVING OFF THE BAD YEAR BLIMP. OR RATHER, I ENTERED THE WORLD OF *DOOKIE*, AND GREEN DAY FOUND ME.

CHAPTER THREE

SKELETONS COME TO LIFE
IN MY CLOSET

MY GREAT-GRANDMOTHER, MIMITA, WAS THE MATRIARCH OF THE FAMILY. I WAS SURE THAT MY FAMILY HAD CREATED THEIR OWN VERSION OF MIMITA'S VALUE SYSTEM, IN ORDER TO FIT THEIR MORE CONVENTIONAL WORLD. I BELIVED MIMITA WAS SOME SORT OF A PRE-ADOLESCENT EXPLORER — I THOUGHT SHE WAS OKAY WITH HOMOS, SHE JUST DIDN'T TALK ABOUT IT BECAUSE *THE BIBLE* TOLD HER NOT TO. SHE AND I HAD AN ELECTRIC PULSE THAT AMPLIFIED WHEN WE SPOKE. I LIKED TO BELIEVE EVERY MEMBER OF MY FAMILY HAD SOME KIND OF DEEP INTERNAL SYMPATHY FOR HOMOS ... BECAUSE ISN'T THAT WHAT BEING A CUBAN EXILE IS ALL ABOUT?

... CLASPING THE ARMS OF YOUR BROTHERS AND SISTERS WHO WERE DISMISSED BY THE COMMUNIST REVOLUTION BECAUSE OF THEIR IDENTITIES?

GRASPING ONTO YOUR BRETHREN WHOSE STOLEN CULTURE AND IDENTITY WAS, IN FACT, NOT COMPENSATED WITH TAX-FREE BONUSES AND 3-STORY FOUNTAINS ON THEIR FRONT LAWNS, NO MATTER WHAT THEY DID WITH THEIR LIVES?

LA VIRGEN MADE THOSE MALE SAINTS LOOK LIKE HOMOPHOBES, LIKE ROSEANNE BARR MADE ALL OF TELEVISION LOOK MISOGYNIST. IT'S LIKE THEY WERE THESE GREATER ENTITIES WHO ADJUSTED TO THE UNDERSTANDING THAT THERE'S A BILLION KINDS OF

PEOPLE ON EARTH.

I WANTED TO BELIEVE THERE WAS A GLITCH IN THE THINGS WE WERE TAUGHT RATHER THAN THE WAY THAT WE ARE . . .

GOD HATES FAGS

THE BOOK OF LEVITICUS (2ND EDITION)

THE FEDERALIST PAPERS

IN DEFENSE OF THE RIGHT

REPUBLICAN REVOLUTION

BANNED
FOR INACCURACY

SO I NEVER FOUGHT BACK; I JUST SAT BACK, SCARED AND ANGRY AND HOLDING ONTO MYSELF . . .

ABOUT THE "BISEXUAL WHO SPREAD DISEASES," ABOUT THE "DISGUSTING LESBIANS WHO DO DISGUSTING THINGS IN ORDER TO ATTRACT ATTENTION," ABOUT THE "SICK PEOPLE WHO REJECT THE GENDER THEY WERE ASSIGNED AT BIRTH," ABOUT "THE DISGUSTING HOMOSEXUALS WHO LURE YOU INTO THEIR HAUNTING GRIP . . .

THERE WAS NO WAY ON EARTH THAT HOMO-SEXUALS COULD BE POWERFUL ENOUGH TO ANGER AN ENTIRE NATION, BECAUSE I FOR ONE USUALLY FELT **FUCKING SILENCED.** BUT I TRIED TO SEE THROUGH REALITY — WHEN I SAT ALONE IN MY CLOSET, WHICH I COULD DECORATE AND RE-DECORATE AS OFTEN AS MY SEROTONIN NEEDED A JUMP-START. IN A WAY, I JUSTIFIED MY EXISTENCE THROUGH MIMITA'S PROJECTED WAY OF THINKING.

MIMITA PASSED AWAY WHEN I WAS ABOUT 8 YEARS OLD. I HAD MY OWN CONSTRUCTED REALITY THEN, WHEN I STILL LIVED IN A CARDBOARD BOX, AND EVERYTHING FELT SECURE.

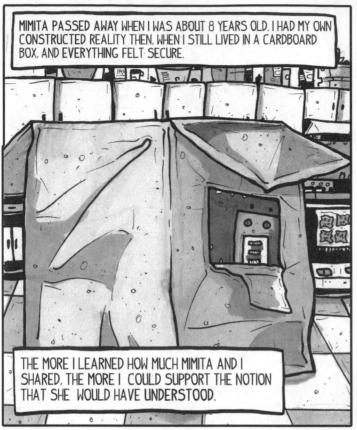

THE MORE I LEARNED HOW MUCH MIMITA AND I SHARED, THE MORE I COULD SUPPORT THE NOTION THAT SHE WOULD HAVE UNDERSTOOD.

MIMITA KEPT CANDY IN A TIN IN HER DRAWER . . .

AND ONE OF HER FAVORITE PASTIMES WAS WATCHING BOXING MATCHES ON TELEVISION . . .

I TOO HID THE FORBIDDEN SUGAR, LEFTOVER FROM SEVERAL HALLOWEENS AGO.

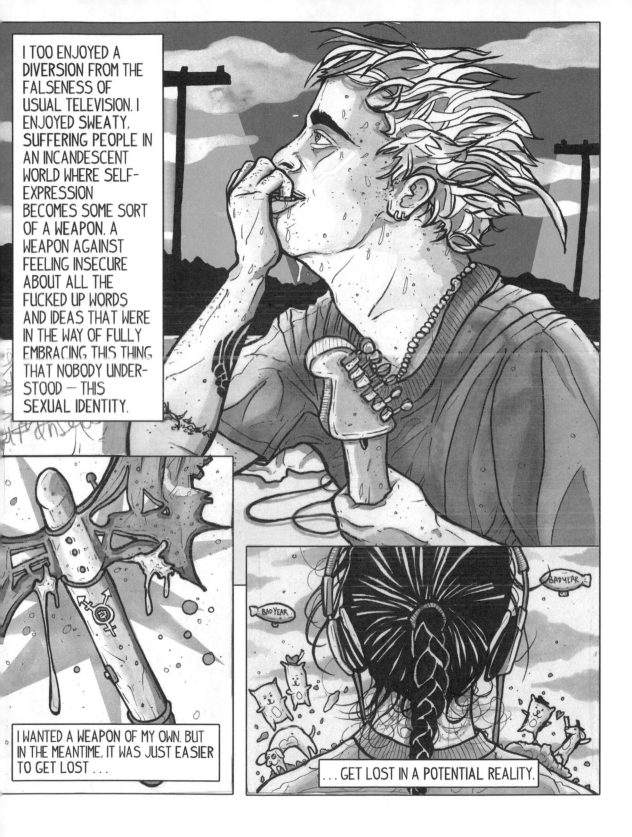

I TOO ENJOYED A DIVERSION FROM THE FALSENESS OF USUAL TELEVISION. I ENJOYED SWEATY, SUFFERING PEOPLE IN AN INCANDESCENT WORLD WHERE SELF-EXPRESSION BECOMES SOME SORT OF A WEAPON. A WEAPON AGAINST FEELING INSECURE ABOUT ALL THE FUCKED UP WORDS AND IDEAS THAT WERE IN THE WAY OF FULLY EMBRACING THIS THING THAT NOBODY UNDER-STOOD — THIS SEXUAL IDENTITY.

I WANTED A WEAPON OF MY OWN. BUT IN THE MEANTIME, IT WAS JUST EASIER TO GET LOST . . .

. . . GET LOST IN A POTENTIAL REALITY.

APRIL 1994

IT WAS SPRING OF 1994 AND I WASN'T EVEN SURE THAT ANYONE COULD SEE THE PROCESS OF REINVENTION THAT I WAS UNDERGOING. THE CLOSEST I REMEMBER COMING TO EXPRESSING MY IDENTITY AROUND MY FAMILY WAS WHEN WE WOULD GET TAKE OUT FROM KFC. I FELT FULL WHEN I WOULD REQUEST THE HOT WINGS BE-CAUSE ACCORDING TO THE COMMERCIAL, *HOT WINGS WERE FOOD FOR MEN.* IN MY REPEATED ATTEMPTS TO BALANCE MY MASCULINITY, I CONSTANTLY SLIPPED IN THE TWO NEW WORDS THAT WOULD DEFINE THE NEXT SHARP TURN MY REPRESENTATION WAS DUE TO TAKE: GREEN *AND* DAY.

GREEN DAY FELT REAL AND TANGIBLE. SO I WONDERED IF THERE WAS MORE BEYOND THEIR MUSIC, IN THEIR PUNK ROCK SCENE? THINGS THAT EXISTED BEFORE GREEN DAY FELL INTO THE CIRCUIT OF POLISHED FLESH, SCULPTED TORSOS, AND HOLLYWOOD?

PERHAPS THERE WAS MORE OUT THERE? MORE SALVATION BESIDES A SINGLE SONG THAT I COULD MOLD MYSELF INTO, AN OLD SONG, A CARTOON ABOUT FARTING, OR A BODILY SENSATION THAT JUSTIFIED MY CLAIMS ON HUMANITY? PERHAPS IT WILL FIND ME?

ALTHOUGH WHATEVER IT MAY BE, I WAS CERTAIN IT WAS NOTHING LIKE GREEN DAY.

I HAD FOUND MYSELF. I THINK ALL I DID THAT WHOLE SUMMER WAS FIND MYSELF OVER AND OVER AGAIN. THE SUMMER OF 1994 . . . I LISTENED TO GREEN DAY EVERY DAY, UNTIL MY EARS BLED.

SOMETIMES I PUT ON THE *LION KING* SOUNDTRACK, OR *GET A GRIP*, IN ORDER TO CALM MYSELF; BUT STILL, THOSE MOMENTS WERE UNDOUBTEDLY FOLLOWED BY A 39TH ROTATION OF *DOOKIE* BY GREEN DAY.

I KNEW THIS WAS THE ULTIMATE INITIATIVE BEHIND SELF-ASSURANCE — FINDING A FAVORITE BAND. A LOT OF PEOPLE HAD BOYFRIENDS, OR SEX, OR MONEY, OR POPULAR-ITY, OR SPORTS: AN IDENTITY BASED ON ABILITY OR LOVE, RATHER THAN UNSUSPECTED PASSION. THIS PASSION EVOKED ABILITIES, BECAUSE GREEN DAY MADE ME WANT TO BE SOMEONE.

GREEN DAY SEEMED TO HAVE PERFECTED THE ART OF POP PUNK. POP PUNK WAS A HYBRID GENRE OF PUNK ROCK, INFLUENCED BY LATE 70s/EARLY 80s POWER POP; AND THE DRIVING RHYTHMS OF MELODIC PUNK ROCK LIKE THE RAMONES AND THE SEX PISTOLS. GREEN DAY GATHERED THEIR OWN INFLUENCES FROM LO-FI ALTERNATIVE ROCK LIKE THE REPLACEMENTS AND HUSKER DU, PIC, CLASSIC METAL LIKE BLACK SABBATH, AND THEIR OWN PUNK ROCK HEROES LIKE CRIMPSHRINE, BIKINI KILL, AND OPERATION IVY. I HAD NEVER HEARD ANY OF THESE BANDS BESIDES BLACK SABBATH (I HAD JUST READ ABOUT THEM IN GREEN DAY BIOGRAPHIES, AND LET'S GET REAL, THE ONLY REASON I CAME TO KNOW OZZY'S "CHANGES" WAS BECAUSE BILLIE JOE SEEMED TO ALWAYS BREAK INTO IT DURING THE INTERMISSION AT GREEN DAY SHOWS). BUT I WAS EAGER AND PASSIONATE ABOUT INVESTIGATING IT ALL. GREEN DAY, BASICALLY, SOUNDED AS IF BROADWAY MUSICALS WERE PUNK, AS IF TELEVISION THEME SONGS WERE ANGRY, AND AS IF THE WORLD WAS REJOICING IN FOOLISH MERRIMENT...
ALL THE WHILE OWNING OUR SELF-LOATHING TENDENCIES.

ALL OF GREEN DAY WERE MODERATELY SIZED MEN, ALWAYS REPEATING THEIR OUTFITS, AND WILDLY COVERED IN SCARS AND BLEMISHES. I HAD NOT SEEN THAT ON TELEVISION, UNLESS IT WAS SOME KIND OF "BEFORE" PHOTO IN A SKIN-CREAM INFOMERCIAL. BESIDES FAVORING MY NEED FOR DEEP CHORUSES, BILLIE JOE'S LYRICS WERE HONING MY EMERGING SELF-AWARENESS. ON "COMING CLEAN," *11:03 (SONG 11, VERSE 3), IN THE BOOK OF DOOKIE; BILLIE JOE CASUALLY REFERENCES PARENTS' MISUNDERSTANDING OF SEXUALITY — OUR NEW DEFINITIONS OF GENDER VERSUS THEIR PRE-DISPOSED ONES.

SO, I WAS OFFICIALLY SOLD, AND THESE IDEAS, FROM THE ATTIC OF MY MIND AND FORBIDDEN GOALS, WERE BECOMING REAL, AS IF ONE CAN ACTUALLY COME OUT OF THE CLOSET AND SURVIVE; AND IT'S NOT JUST SOMETHING YOU SEE IN AFTER-SCHOOL DOCUMENTARIES ABOUT ALTERNATIVE LIFESTYLES. IT'S SOMETHING THAT CAN HAPPEN TO ANYONE — PUNK ROCK GUYS, PUNK ROCK GIRLS, PEOPLE WHO HAVE NEVER HEARD OF PUNK ROCK, AN ESTRANGED CUBANITA, TU HIJA. ALL OF A SUDDEN, I COULD LOOK BEYOND THE OLDER GENERATION'S ORTHO-CATHOLIC SOCIALIZATION AND HOLD TIGHTLY, WITH MY DEAR LIFE, TO A NEW SOCIALIZATION — THE ONE I CREATED THROUGH THE WORDS OF GREEN DAY.

I DID NOT UNDERSTAND THIS FEELING OF MUSIC SETTLING ITSELF INTERNALLY, TO THE POINT WHERE I COULD FEEL EMOTIONALLY OKAY, AT LEAST FOR THE TIME BEING. I DID NOT KNOW I WAS STILL CAPABLE OF THE KIND OF INSPIRATION THAT HAPPENED DURING CHILDHOOD WHEN YEYA SANG "LOS POLLITOS" AT THE BEGINNING OF THE DAY.

UPON THIS SELF-LOVE, I BECAME INDIFFERENT TO THE THINGS ON EARTH THAT CHALLENGED MY EXISTENCE, BECAUSE I HAD THIS *"OTHER."* I WOULD'VE LIKED TO HAVE A BEST FRIEND OR A BOYFRIEND OR A GIRLFRIEND OR WHATEVER, BUT FOR THE TIME BEING I HAD A FAVORITE BAND. AND I COULD DEFINITELY POINT OUT A FEW THINGS I COULD LEARN FROM THIS, AND NOT FROM A BOYFRIEND, INCLUDING (BUT NOT LIMITED TO) THE RECLAMATION OF SELF.

I WAS GAY. I NOTED FOR THE FIRST TIME TO MYSELF, WITH CERTAINTY, A FIST ON THE TABLE, AND A HOLY CROSS SOBBING OVER A LITTLE SAUCER OF HOLY WATER. I WAS GOING TO STAY THIS WAY, AND I HOPED TO CONTINUE NOT TO CARE. I PLEDGED TO CONTINUE TO DELVE INTO THE UNFOLDED CIRCUITS OF GREEN DAY AND FURTHER MY QUEST. BECAUSE WHILE HUMANITY CREATED EXISTENCE, GREEN DAY EXPLAINED A LIFE I WANTED TO CREATE FOR MYSELF— AN UNDERWORLD WHERE PEOPLE LIKE ME COULD EXIST.

MY KNOWLEDGE WAS LIMITED, ALTHOUGH I KNEW GREEN DAY TOOK PANSY DIVISION, AN ALL-GAY POP PUNK BAND FROM BERKELEY, CA, ON THEIR FIRST TOUR IN SUPPORT OF *DOOKIE*.

THEY, IN FACT, DID NOT TAKE PEARL JAM.

I STILL HAD NOT FOUND ACCESS TO THESE QUEER PUNK ICONS WHO I SAW REFERENCED IN EVERYTHING THAT SURROUNDED GREEN DAY. AND I WONDERED IF THAT WAS AN IDENTITY I COULD ACTUALLY PURSUE — BEING A MEMBER OF A CREATIVE CIRCUIT EXCLUDED FROM THE MAINSTREAM AND EMBRACING OF THE DICK-SUCKING, PUSSY-LICKING, HUMANIZING, FUCKED-UP-NESS OF HUMANITY . . .

SO I BELIEVED I WOULD FIND THAT COMMUNITY ONE DAY -- WHEN THE RIGHT PERSON OR NEWSPAPER OR RADIO SHOW OR CATACLYSMIC MOMENT REMINDED ME TO KEEP MOVING ALTHOUGH EVERYTHING MIGHT BE FALLING APART.   AS I GREW, I LEARNED THE LIMITATIONS OF MY OWN SURROUNDINGS — WHERE MY FAMILY WAS COMING FROM, THE DEMONS WE WERE FIGHTING AGAINST, AND WHAT WE SHOULD DO IN ORDER TO UNDERSTAND THE WAYS IN WHICH LIFE HAD AFFECTED US. FAMILY WAS A UNIT WITH FRAGILE BEARINGS BECAUSE THE CYCLE OF LIFE INEVITABLY INCLUDES DECEIT, DIVORCE, DIFFERENCES, AND EVENTUALLY, DETERMINATION.

MY FAMILY SEEMED TO BE ABLE TO REST NOW. THEY KNEW THAT I HAD FOUND GREEN DAY, AND FOR SOME REASON, WHATEVER WAS DEBILITATING MY ABILITY TO SEEM OUTWARDLY ENTHUSIASTIC ABOUT BEING ALIVE WAS NO LONGER IN THE WAY.

CHAPTER FOUR

AM I PARANOID?
OR AM I JUST BI?

I STARTED SEVENTH GRADE AT A NEW SCHOOL,
MARINA HERNANDEZ JUNIOR HIGH, IN SEPTEMBER OF 1994.
IT WAS JUST THE FIRST DAY, BUT THE GENDER-BASED
SUBMISSION HAD ALREADY BEGUN. BASICALLY, WE ALL
GOT GENDERED GIFT BAGS -- THE GIRLS RECEIVED SECRET
BRAND DEODORANT AND MASCARA, AND THE GUYS
RECEIVED SPEED STICK AND CHEWING GUM. I WAS
IMMEDIATELY
OFFENDED AND
BURIED MY GIFTS
AT THE BOTTOM
OF MY BACKPACK
IN CASE I EVER
NEEDED THEM.
FOR NOW, I
CHOSE TO
REMAIN
PARTIALLY
INSECURE.

I SUCKED MY THUMB ALL THROUGH MIDDLE SCHOOL. IT MADE MOST PEOPLE CONFUSED, BUT MY FAMILY SEEMED TO FIND IT CUTE AND ENTERTAINING. SO, I THOUGHT "WHAT-FUCKING-EVER" WHEN ANYONE CAUGHT ME AT MID-SUCK AND JUDGED ME FOR SUCKING MY THUMB AT 12 YEARS OLD.

DESPITE THESE INEVITABLE INSECURITIES THAT CAME WITH BEING A GAY CUBAN GIRL IN 1994 — I KNEW THAT I WAS MATURE NOW.

NOW THAT I HAD FOUND A FAVORITE BAND — AN IDENTITY.

GRANTED, REALITY WAS CONSTRICTED — WHETHER OR NOT I USED THESE TOOLS TO METICULOUSLY MOLD MY SELF CONFIDENCE. BECAUSE DEEP INSIDE, I STILL FELT LIKE LA RARITA — LA TORTILLERA. I COULD NOT BE MYSELF ON A DAY-TO-DAY BASIS. I COULD NOT BE FULLY FREE . . .

BUT I WOULD TRY TO BE AS FREE AS I COULD. CONTAINED, BUT FREE — TRYING NOT TO TURN MY SOUL AND BRAIN TO DUST.

MY FIRST CLASS THAT DAY WAS GEOGRAPHY WITH MS. NAVARRO. I STEPPED INTO CLASS, SAW MS. NAVARRO, AND WAS SWEPT INTO A WHIRLWIND. I COULD SWEAT, GIGGLE, AND BURN ON THE INSIDE BUT GOD FORBID I SHOW IT ON THE OUTSIDE.

THE MILD EMBARASSMENT MADE ME EXCITED AND COMFORTABLE WITH MY CARNAL URGES. I FELT ALONE — BUT I FELT RIGHT. AND FROM THEN ON, I LOVED GEORGRAPHY. I WANTED TO LEARN — IN SCHOOL — AND THINK ABOUT THE EARTH AND WHY IT WAS THE WAY IT WAS.

IT MADE SENSE. I COULD PULL DOWN THE MAP, BRING MS. NAVARRO AN APPLE, AND ASK HER ABOUT THE BAY AREA. I COULD ASK HER WHERE RODEO IS, SINCE BILLIE JOE AND MIKE DIRNT WERE ORIGINALLY FROM THERE. I COULD ASK HER IF SHE EVEN LIKES GREEN DAY, ALTHOUGH I WAS SURE SHE WAS INTO WHATEVER WAS PLAYING ON EL SOL 95 ...

OR, WHATEVER MOST YOUNG, CONVENTIONAL, ATTRACTIVE CUBAN GIRLS WERE INTO.

I THOUGHT I HAD PROGRESSED AS A PERSON BUT I STILL FELT STUPID, OR FAKE, OR PROCESSED. LIKE HERE I WAS — 8 HOURS OF THE DAY, SURROUNDED BY STRANGERS — AND NOBODY KNOWS THAT I AM GAY. I GUESS THEY WOULD SLIP IN THE OCCASIONAL SHADY COMMENTS ABOUT MY MASCULINITY, BECAUSE NOBODY IGNORES A GIRL WITH A MUSTACHE, BUT AS A GEMINI, WOULD I ACTUALLY FEEL BETTER IF I EXPOSED THE FULL PACKAGE? SO FAR, I WAS NOT DOING ANYTHING TO QUESTION THINGS LIKE THE GOVERNMENT AND THE BIBLE THROUGH MY PHYSICAL IDENTITY.... BESIDES WEARING A FLANNEL SHIRT, REFUSING TO WASH MY HAIR, AND BUYING SHOES IN THE BOYS' SECTION AT PAYLESS.

HEY EVERYONE I'M A BIG HOMO

I ALWAYS WAITED IMPATIENTLY FOR THE END OF THE DAY WHEN I COULD CHOOSE TO BE A SELF-QUESTIONING ADULT, OR A KID WHO LIVED WITH THEIR PARENTS. ALL I WANTED WAS 3 P.M. AND A MOMENT WITH MY SUBCONSCIOUS. I COULD TAKE PRIDE IN PUNK ROCK, ITS POLITICAL INCLINATIONS, AND ALL THE THINGS I HAD READ ABOUT THAT SUDDENLY.

HUMANIZED (AND SOMETIMES, TO M CONFLICTING DISMAY, FETISHIZED) M "ALTERNATIVE LIFESTYLE. FOR NOW, UNINTERRUPTED THOUGHT ABOUT THE FUTURE WERE M ESCAPE, AS LONG AS SCHOO CONTINUED TO FORCE ME INT CHOOSING THE DECIMAL SYSTE OVER SCHEMING M GENDER IDENTIT

ALTERNATIVE TO WHAT? WAS SCRIBBLED ON MY GEOGRAPHY CLASS FOLDER (BILLIE JOE ARMSTRONG SAID THAT ONCE ON MTV) IN REFERENCE TO SOMETHING OTHER THAN MY SEXUAL ORIENTATION; BUT STILL, IT WAS THE WORD USAGE. THE USE OF "ALTERNATIVE" AND ITS UNIFIED DEFINITION OF OTHERNESS. OTHERNESS TO WHAT, EXACTLY? CALLING IT AN ALTERNATIVE LIFESTYLE MADE IT SOUND LIKE THIS CHOICE WE MADE TO LIVE DIFFERENTLY, AS IF WE HAD OTHER OPTIONS. BUT DEEP INSIDE I WAS A BIG HOMO, POUNDING TO COME OUT, WITH ZERO CHOICES . . . JUST DESIRES, WHICH WERE HAPLESSLY FALLING APART. AND WHY SHOULD OUR OTHERNESS MATTER, TO THE POINT THAT WE'RE ALTERNATIVE? NEVERTHELESS I DECIDED TO OWN WHATEVER WOULD EXAMINE THE STATUS QUO, AND EMBRACE THIS ALTERNATIVEDOM AS AN ACCESSIBLE IDENTITY I COULD USE TO EXPLAIN TO THE REST OF THE WORLD WHEN THEY ASKED ME WHY I LOOKED THE WAY I LOOKED. I COULD SIGH OR HOLD MY BREATH AND EXCUSE MY LIES. I COULD SAY THAT I'M JUST "ALTERNATIVE" AND THAT'S ALL THEY SHOULD REALLY WORRY ABOUT.

AT MARINA I WAS STILL THE GIRL WITH THE SIDEBURNS AND THE LITTLE MUSTACHE.

NOT MUCH HAD CHANGED AND KIDS WERE STILL PRETTY RUDE HUMAN BEINGS. SO I ASSOCIATED WITH FEW. I FAVORED THEIR INTEREST IN GREEN DAY, WHETHER OR NOT IT MEANT BATTLING MY WAY THROUGH EYEBROW-RELATED INSULTS BY COMPARING MYSELF TO BILL BARRY FROM R.E.M.

I SEARCHED NEAR AND FAR FOR THE ALTERNA-TEENS WHO MAY UNDERSTAND. JENNY, LEILA, BART, AND EDDY VALIDATED MY ABILITY TO MAKE NEW FRIENDS. BUT BY OCTOBER, EVERYONE HAD ALREADY CHOSEN TLC, ADINA HOWARD, NINE INCH NAILS — AND SUBTLE NORMALCY — OVER GREEN DAY.

YEAH, I GET IT. "WATERFALLS" IS AN AMAZING SONG WITH AN INCREDIBLY POWERFUL MESSAGE. I FOUND IT SO TERRIBLY IMPORTANT THAT THIS SONG EXISTED, BUT I DIDN'T SEE THE POINT IN MAKING FUN OF ME OVER THE FACT THAT IT WON OVER GREEN DAY'S "BASKET CASE" FOR VIDEO OF THE YEAR AT THE 1994 MTV VIDEO MUSIC AWARDS.

I OFTEN FELT LIKE A CREATURE OF NO ASSUMED GENDER OR AGE. SOMETIMES I LOVED BEING THAT CREATURE, BUT EVERYONE ELSE JUST LAUGHED IN SHOCK AND AWE AT MY JOKES ABOUT SEX OR BOOGERS, WHICH WAS JUST ABOUT WHERE MOST LOOMING CONNECTIONS WOULD END—AT THE TAIL END OF AN AWKWARD PUNCH LINE ABOUT MASTURBATION. I COULD SEE A LIMIT AS TO HOW MUCH OF A GIRL I COULD BE ACCEPTED AS BY THE GIRLS, AND HOW MUCH OF A BOY I COULD BE ACCEPTED AS BY THE BOYS. THE DISCORD PUSHED ME TOWARD CENSORSHOP . . . SILENCE . . . DEATH.

WHEN THE JOKES WERE OVER, I SPENT A LOT OF MY TIME HOLDING MY BREATH.

IT SEEMED LIKE MY FAVORITE THING WAS TO SIT IN MS. NAVARRO'S CLASS AND DECONSTRUCT THE CHRONOLOGY OF MY GENDER IDENTITY, DOODLE AFTER DOODLE. I ALWAYS RESORT- ED TO THINKING ABOUT DENICE. SHE WAS THE POPULAR TOMBOY IN GRADE SCHOOL. NOBODY SEEMED TO CRITICIZE HER MASCULINITY BE- CAUSE EVERYONE LOVED A GOOD ATHLETE. EVERYONE LOVED A WELL- SPOKEN TOMBOY WITH A GOOD SENSE OF HUMOR, BLOND HAIR, AND A BOYFRIEND. SHE HAD THIS FRIEND, SABRINA, WHO WAS PRETTY COOL AND ALSO NICE TO ME. SABRINA HELPED US BE FRIENDS; BUT I THOUGHT DENICE FELT DEEPLY SORRY FOR ME.

I WANTED TO LIKE BOTH HER AND MY VERSION OF TOMBOYHOOD, BUT I HATED MY LACK OF ATHLETIC ABILITY. I HATED CARING IF MY HAIR HAD BEEN WASHED AND IF IT OFFENDED ANYONE. I HATED CARING IF MY OUTFIT WAS FEMININE ENOUGH, IF MY ANDROGYNY WAS BEING SEEN AS A PHASE, AND IF I LOOKED TOO GAY FROM WEARING THE THINGS THAT HELPED ME FEEL SANE AND ALIVE.

AND THEN, THERE WAS ALWAYS THOSE SHIRTS-- THE ONES I WORE ON CLASS PHOTO DAY. I STOPPED COMPROMISING FOR PICTURE DAY SINCE I STARTED JUNIOR HIGH, BUT IT'S THE SCAR THAT COUNTS. I CALLED THESE SHIRTS PUNISHMENT SHIRTS, AS FORCED FEMININITY OFTEN FELT AS SUCH. PUNISHMENT SHIRTS WERE THE BANE OF MY EXISTENCE WHEN VISUAL REPRESENTATION WAS ALL I HAD TO GIVE A MILD, AND MAYBE EVEN COMFORTING SUGGESTION THAT I VERY WELL MAY BE A HOMOSEXUAL.

SABRINA EXECUTED THESE VERY EXCITING WAYS OF LOOKING AT THE THINGS I HATED -- BECAUSE EVERYTHING I HATED MADE HER HAPPY. I USED TO WEAR THAT SHIRT I HATED BECAUSE SHE SAID SHE LIKED IT. I REMEMBER HOW TERRIBLE IT WAS THAT IT FELT SO GOOD TO MAKE HER SMILE. I WONDER IF SHE STILL LIKES SPORTS OR IF SHE REALIZED SHE WAS BETTER OFF PLAYING VIDEO GAMES? I HELD ON TO THIS ONE MOMENT WHERE THE GAP WAS BRIDGED BECAUSE DENICE CALLED ME A TOMBOY. IN LINE, WE HAD TO STAND BOY/GIRL/BOY/GIRL. DENICE SUGGESTED THAT WE ELIMNATE THE BOYS FROM BETWEEN US, SINCE, AFTER ALL, THE THREE OF US WERE HALF-BOYS.

I WONDERED HOW MANY PEOPLE ASSUMED I MIGHT EVEN BE GAY. AND WHETHER OR NOT THEIR DISCONNECT HAD MORE TO DO WITH THAT AND LESS TO DO WITH TLC WRITING BETTER MUSIC THAN GREEN DAY. I STARTED TO PANIC ABOUT WHERE TO STASH THE INEVITABLE FEAR OF BEING OUT, BECAUSE I WAS STARTING TO WILT, SLOWLY, FROM CLAUSTROPHOBIA.

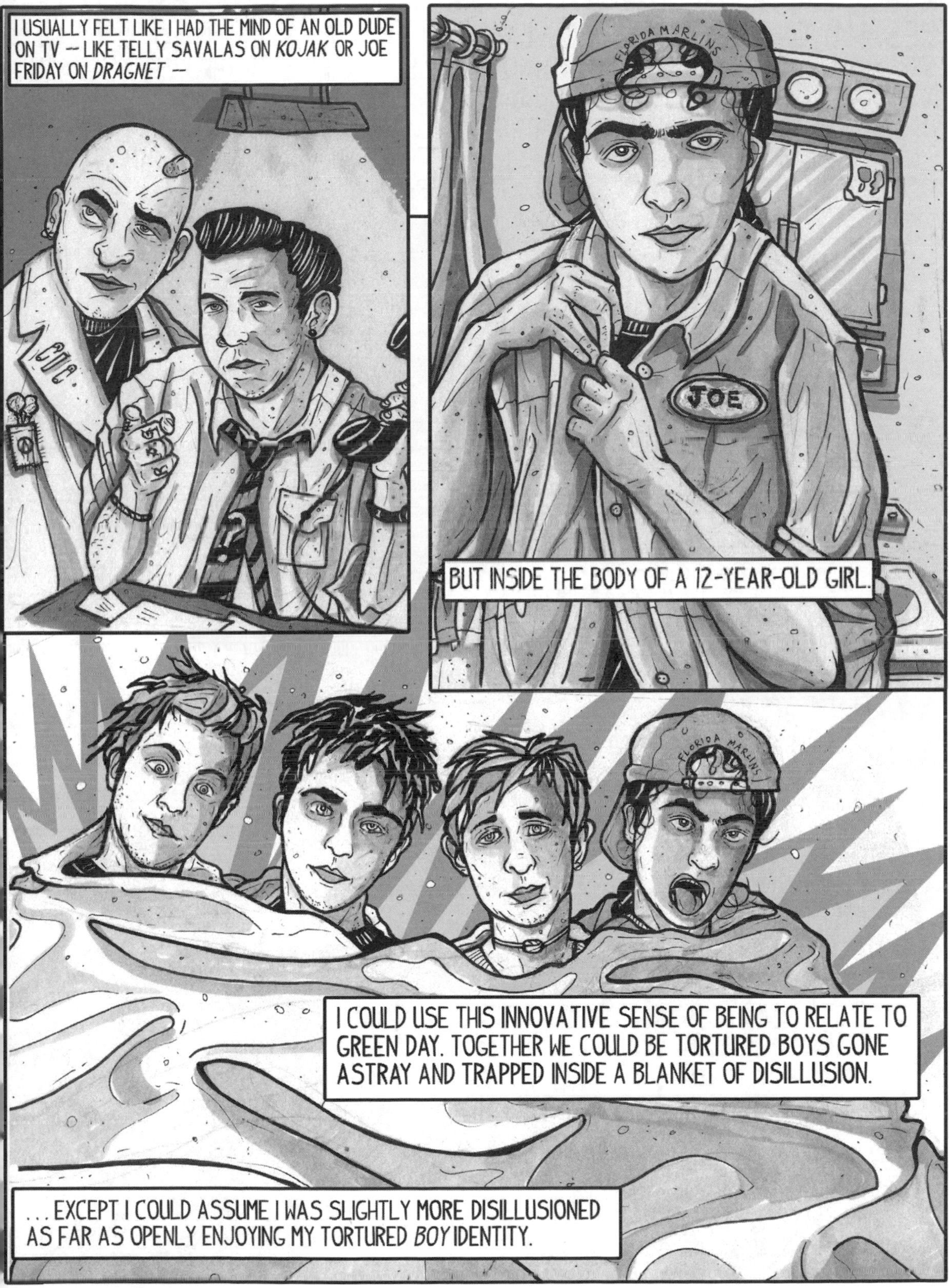
I USUALLY FELT LIKE I HAD THE MIND OF AN OLD DUDE ON TV — LIKE TELLY SAVALAS ON KOJAK OR JOE FRIDAY ON DRAGNET —
CTC
FLORIDA MARLINS
JOE
BUT INSIDE THE BODY OF A 12-YEAR-OLD GIRL.
FLORIDA MARLINS
I COULD USE THIS INNOVATIVE SENSE OF BEING TO RELATE TO GREEN DAY. TOGETHER WE COULD BE TORTURED BOYS GONE ASTRAY AND TRAPPED INSIDE A BLANKET OF DISILLUSION.
. . . EXCEPT I COULD ASSUME I WAS SLIGHTLY MORE DISILLUSIONED AS FAR AS OPENLY ENJOYING MY TORTURED BOY IDENTITY.

NOTHING EXCITED ME MORE THAN A LONG DRIVE ACROSS THE PALMETTO EX-
PRESSWAY ON A DREARY GRAY EVENING. THE PALM TREES RUSTLED TO THE SOUND OF
EGRETS AND THE FRESH AROMA OF BIRTHING SWAMP LIFE WOULD SEEP THROUGH THE CRACK IN
MY WINDOW. THE MORE I LEARNED OF THE BAY AREA IN CALIFORNIA, THE LESS I LIKED FLORIDA.
BUT THE MORE I EXITED MY INTERPLANETARY CONFINES AND LOOKED OUT MY WINDOW, THE MORE I
WANTED TO REINVENT MY PERSPECTIVE. FOR NOW, IT WAS THE
MOST EXCITING THING WHEN MAMA HAD TO RUN AN ERRAND AFTER
WORK. I COULD LISTEN TO GREEN DAY AND STARE AT A
MOVING SKY AS OPPOSE TO A CONCRETE WALL.

FARM
STORES

EXPRESS

HOT BREAD
EMPANADAS
ALL DAY

PAYLESS   LUPA SHOES   CARVEL

THE STATIC BETWEEN ADULTHOOD AND PRE-TEEN ENSLAVEMENT SEEMED OBSOLETE
BECAUSE I WAS FREE ON THIS ROAD WITH MY THOUGHTS, AN EVER-CHANGING
VIEW, AND THE ABILITY
TO SIT WITH MYSELF.

INSIDE THAT COCOON OF FILTH WHERE THE ONLY INHABITANTS WERE ME AND MY QUESTIONS ABOUT SURVIVAL, I THOUGHT ABOUT THE FUTURE AND HOW MY BODY MIGHT TAKE FORM — WITHOUT CHECKING IN WITH MY SUBCONCIOUS.

DAYDREAMED ABOUT WHAT MY BODY WOULD LOOK LIKE IN THE FUTURE, BUT WAS OKAY WITH WHAT HAD. FOR NOW, MY INSECURITIES COWERED BEHIND A BUTCH SMILE THAT I COULD SHOW OFF HENEVER I DIDN'T KNOW WHAT TO SAY.

I WAS USUALLY UNCOMFORTABLE WITH MY HAIR, MY PROPORTIONS, THE SPEED MY TITS WERE GROWING AT, AND THE SHAPE OF MY FACE. STILL, I LEARNED IT WAS WORTH TRYING TO SELF-RIGHTEOUSLY OWN THE THINGS THAT I WANTED TO LOVE — THE THINGS NO ONE ELSE SEEMED TO UNDERSTAND. BECUASE WHEN I WAS ALONE, I WAS STILL IN MY FAVORITE SHIRT, MY FAVORITE SHOES, AND FOR NOW . . .

. . . MY ONLY BODY.

THE MIND SHIFTS TOO OFTEN TO CHOOSE A PATH OF SAFETY. AND BETWEEN ME AND GREEN DAY, I DIDN'T REALLY CARE WHETHER OR NOT I WOULD DECIDE TO PUT ON SHREDDED FISHNETS, SHITTY DAY-GLO LIPSTICK AND THE MASCARA FROM THE SIXTH-GRADE GIFT BAG THAT WAS COLLECTING DUST ON MY BATHROOM WINDOWSILL. THE PROBLEM WASN'T IN THE PATH TO GENDER BENEDICTION, BUT IN SOCIETY'S INABILITY TO MAKE FEMININITY ACCESSIBLE — AN OPTION RATHER THAN THE ONLY CHOICE, A CHOICE THAT'S ONLY AVAILABLE TO YOU AFTER YOU'VE FOLLOWED A SERIES OF EXERCISES.

SO WHY NOT APPEND THE MEDIA'S PORTRAYAL OF OVERSEXUALIZED FEMININITY? APPEND THE EMBRACE OF OVERSEXUALIZED FEMALE MASCULINITY? REPRESENT WOMEN WHO LOOK DIFFERENT. WOMEN OF DIFFERENT SHAPES. MASCULINE WOMEN. SENSITIVE MEN. TOUGH PEOPLE WITH NO VISIBLE GENDER, WEARING NOTHING BUT THEIR HEARTS ON THEIR SLEEVES. PEOPLE WHO ARE NOT DEFINED BY THEIR SEXUALITY.

THE MEMBERS OF GREEN DAY WERE NOT IN RELATIONSHIPS WITH FASHION MODELS. GRANTED, IF THEY EVER DECIDE TO DO THAT SORT OF THING, TO EACH THEIR OWN, RIGHT? BUT FOR NOW, THEIR RELATIONSHIPS ARE INTERCONNECTED WITH THE HUMBLENESS OF THEIR PUNK UPBRINGING. FOR NOW, I THOUGHT I HAD DEFINED THE SENSATION, WHICH CAME FROM GREEN DAY'S COMMUNITY. I KNEW THAT FOR ME, THIS POLITICALLY CHARGED, OUTWARDLY GAY, EAST BAY PUNK SCENE EMITTED A SENSE OF HOME. I CAME TO UNDERSTAND THE PRECIOUSNESS OF EVADING THE MAIN-STREAM, BUT IT PAINED ME TO KNOW WHAT GREEN DAY HAD TO COMPROMISE IN ORDER TO EMBRACE FINANCIAL STABILITY. THE FEELING I GOT FROM IMAGERY AND RECOLLECTIONS OF GREEN DAY'S BIRTHING GROUND WAS SIMILAR TO THE FEELING I GOT FROM WATCHING *THE MUPPETS TAKE MANHATTAN* IN 1987. IT WAS THE SAME SUBTLE WARMTH THAT SENT SHIVERS UP MY SPINE EVERY TIME I STARED INTO THE DEPTHS OF TRASH GRACEFULLY PILED ALONG BILLIE JOE AND HIS WIFE ADRIENNE ON THEIR WEDDING PHOTO.

IT WAS THE SAME FEELING I GOT WHEN THERE WAS A NEW EPISODE OF *REN & STIMPY*. THE SAME FEELING I GOT WHEN I FANTASIZED ABOUT THE FUTURE, NOW THAT I THOUGHT I MAY HAVE FOUND ONE. I ADMIRED THE WAY THAT GREEN DAY STILL EMITTED THIS FEELING OF HOME THROUGH THE WORDS AND MUSIC THEY HAD RELEASED WITHOUT ARTISTIC COMPROMISE, WHETHER OR NOT THEY HAD LOST EVERYTHING ELSE (ACCORDING TO *HIT PARADER* MAGAZINE).

I CRADLED THIS NEW IDEA THAT SEXUALITY CAN BE APPRECIATED, AND WE CAN LOVE OURSELVES, EXERT OURSELVES PHYSICALLY, FEEL ATTRACTIVE, AND FIND LOVE WITHOUT SUBMITTING TO THE HETEROCENTRIC PARADIGM. LOVE CAN MANIFEST AS THIS OFFBEAT THING THAT I HAD NOT BEFORE CONSIDERED, WHEN I HAD CONVINCED MYSELF LOVE WAS NOT FOR PEOPLE LIKE ME. THIS WORLD WHERE THIS LOVE COULD EXIST REMAINED A FANTASY, LIKE A PROSPECT -- WHEN I WOULD GATHER THE NOTION THAT IT MAY VERY WELL STILL EXIST BEYOND GREEN DAY, SOMEWHERE . . . SOMEWHERE, OUT THERE, GAY PUNKS ARE NOT DYING.

SEVENTH GRADE FELT AS IF IT WERE DIVIDED BETWEEN GEOGRAPHY CLASS AND NOT-GEOGRAPHY CLASS. TODAY WE WERE LEARNING ABOUT PLATE TECTONICS. THERE WAS SOMETHING IN THE WAY MS. NAVARRO SAID *PLATE TECTONICS*, SOMETHING POWERFUL AND HONEST WHEN SHE POINTED TO THE SAN FRANCISCO BAY AREA ON HER PULL-DOWN MAP. I FELT SECURE IN HER CLASS, UNTIL MARCO OR LAZ SPIT OUT SOME BULLSHIT ABOUT "FAGGOTS."

"FAGGOT" — THE WORD TERRORIZED ME, DESPITE ITS INCLINATION TOWARD MALES.

THE WORD DRIPPED LIKE **POISON** FROM THEIR MOUTHS EVERYTIME IT WAS SPOKEN.

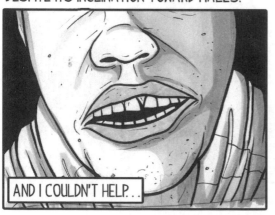

AND I COULDN'T HELP...

...BUT FEEL SILENCED.

IF I GOT A DIME FOR EVERY TIME MARCO OR LAZ CALLED ONE ANOTHER "FAGGOT" WHENEVER EITHER ONE DID ANYTHING MILDLY EMASCULATING (SUCH AS DRINKING OUT OF A FLORAL-PRINTED CUP), I WOULD BE TOTALLY RICH.

...THEN, I WOULD SPEND THE MONEY BRIBING LAZ AND MARCO TO COME OUT OF THE CLOSET AND BECOME MY BEST FRIENDS.

BESIDES THEM, I HAD MADE SOME FRIENDS.

(MARIMAR)

(CLARITA)

IT WAS EASY TO PLACE THE HOMOPHOBES IN MY BLIND SPOT WITH MY TWO NEW FRIENDS BY MY SIDE. MARIMAR WAS A POIGNANT GEMINI AND POSSIBLY THE FIRST SELF-IDENTIFIED FEMINIST I HAD EVER KNOWN. SHE WAS INTO GRUNGE MUSIC AND MYSTERIOUS, DARK POETRY. CLARITA WAS MY CAPRICORN COUNTERPART, WHO BOWED DOWN AT THE FEET OF HER CALLING — NINE INCH NAILS. WE SHARED A SIMILAR HOPELESS FANATICISM FOR OUR HEROES WHO HELPED US MAINTAIN OUR SANITY.

LIKE RELIGIOUS FANATICS, WE HAD FOUND OUR DESTINY, OUR WAYWARD PATH — ALTERNATIVE ROCK.

A DESTINY THAT PROMISED WORLD PEACE, SEX EDUCATION, AND ALTERNATIVE FAMILY VALUES.

OPENLY DROOLING AT THE SIGHT OF A CUTE BOY WAS SOCIALLY ACCEPTABLE, SO I WAS *"SOCIALLY ACCEPTABLE"* WHEN I COULD BE. MARIMAR LIKED THEM INTROSPECTIVE; I LIKED THEM LOUD AND TORTURED,

ALTHOUGH WE BOTH PREFERRED THEM IN FLANNEL WITH SOME UNCONVENTIONAL HAIRCUT AND A FRONT ROW SEAT IN THE ALTERNATIVE ROCK PIGENHOLE. I COULD FEEL THE EVOLUTION IN MY VEINS . . .

EVERY DAY I WOULD CATCH MYSELF OPENLY DROOLING AT THE SIGHT OF ANY ANGRY GIRL OR FEY BOY WHO CROSSED MY PATH. HIDING MY IDENTITY FROM MY NEWFOUND FRIENDS WAS LESS PAINFUL THAN THE REST OF MY CLOSETED INTERACTIONS — BECAUSE SOMETHING TOLD ME I WOULD BE ABLE TO COME OUT TO THEM, AND SOON.

STILL, I WOULD ALWAYS RATHER TALK ABOUT GREEN DAY OR PUNK, AND MARIMAR AND CLARITA LISTENED. IT WAS PECULIAR, THOUGH, TO ACT AS IF MY INTEREST IN BOYS WAS ANY-THING LESS THAN CONVOLUTED . . . THERE WAS THIS ONE PHOTO OF BILLIE JOE, THOUGH. THE CUTE PHOTO THAT WASN'T DIGITALLY ALTERED AND HIS TEETH WERE EVERYWHERE BUT THE INSIDE OF HIS MOUTH AND THE FEMININE CURL OF HIS EYELASHES WERE EXPOSED. IT WAS MY TICKET TO GETTING AWAY WITH CLOSET MURDER.

CLOSET MURDER WAS HARDLY A TRIUMPH. IT IS CHARACTERIZED BY BEING SO GOOD AT BEING IN THE CLOSET, THAT FOOLING THE MASSES BECOMES EASY. I COULD HIDE BEHIND THE OFFHANDED STARES AT THE FEY BOYS, THE INHERENT FOCUS ON PUNK ROCK AS A LIFESTYLE, AND THROUGH THE FACT THAT I HADN'T DEEPLY CRUSHED ON A GIRL YET. A GIRL WHO WASN'T FROM MY PAST. A GIRL WHO WASN'T FAIRUZA BALK, MELISSA JOAN HART, LARISA OLEYNIK ON *THE SECRET WORLD OF ALEX MACK*, OR CHARYTIN. I HAD YET TO MEET AN ACTUAL QUEER. BUT I KNEW THEY WERE OUT THERE SOMEWHERE IN PUNK ROCK. MAYBE SOMEWHERE IN MIAMI BEACH?

UNTI THEN, MY BATHROOM WAS THE SAFEST BET.

MIAMI BEACH OR NOT, I WAS TRYING TO GROW UP. I STARTED LISTENING TO *ONE STEP BEYOND*, A RADIO SHOW ON THE COLLEGE STATION THAT AIRED PUNK AND SKA. I WOULD CALL IN TO REQUEST BANDS THAT I HEARD OF THROUGH GREEN DAY, LIKE PANSY DIVISION AND BLATZ. I FOUND SOMETHING THAT HAD MUTUALLY FOUND ME, BECAUSE EVERY TIME I HEARD SOMETHING NEW, IT FELT RIGHT. I WAS ON A SERIOUS PATH: LIKE I COULD FURTHER TIE THESE FAULTY STRINGS THAT WERE ONCE CALLED ABNORMALITIES TO THE FRAYING ENDS OF MY SUBCULTURAL BELONGING.

MY ATTENTION SPAN HAD FALTERED FOR THE EIGHTH TIME THAT CLASS PERIOD,
SO I TOOK THE HALL PASS AND CLAIMED DIARRHEA. DIARRHEA OF THE SOUL, I
ADMITTED TO MYSELF, AS I WANDERED TOWARD THE FURTHEST BATHROOM.

I HAD ALREADY ROLLED MY EYES METAPHYSICALLY AT TWO DIFFERENT HOMOPHOBIC COMMENTS, BOTH OF WHICH WERE CELEBRATED BY OUR TEACHER, SO I NEEDED A WALK. I WALKED THROUGH THE HALLS AND STEADILY PACED MYSELF, WITH MY HEADPHONES STREAMING "I WANT TO BE ALONE" OFF OF *39/SMOOTH*. I WALKED SLOWLY TO SAVOR THE IRREPLACE-ABLE MOMENTS WHEN I WAS ALONE, SCAVENGING THROUGH THE WORLD THAT FED OFF OF RESTRICTING ME. THESE WERE MY FAVORITE MO-MENTS. THEY STOOD APART FROM THE REST OF MY LIFE BECAUSE I WAS NOT SCARED OF BEING JUDGED; I WAS NOT CONCERNED WITH SAFETY OR ANYONE'S EXPECTATIONS. I WAS NOT ACCOUNTABLE TO ANYONE.

I HAD A HALL PASS, A TICKET TO *FREEDOM* IF I CONCEALED MY DESTINATION AND MY ALTERNATIVE LIFESTYLE. I WAS NOT FOLLOWING ANYTHING BEYOND THE COURSE OF MY OWN VISIONS.

I WALKED FURTHER, TAKING WRONG TURNS, TAKING MY TIME, TAKING CORNERS OFF SIGNS THAT HAD NOTHING TO DO WITH ME, AND PULLING THE STICKY TACK OFF THE BACKS OF POSTER SO I CAN HAVE SOMETHING TO HOLD ON TO.

I STOPPED AND PEERED INTO EACH WINDOW AND EACH OPEN DOOR, LOOKING FOR PEOPLE WHO LOOKED LIKE ME.

I PASSED BY THE COUNSELOR'S OFFICE AND LOOKED THROUGH THE CRACK IN THE DOOR.

MAY I HELP YOU?

UH, SORRY, I'M IN THE WRONG ROOM. SORRY!

I RAN OFF. I STARTED SWEATING AND WONDERING IF I WAS STILL AT MARINA HERNANDEZ JUNIOR HIGH, OR A FUCKED-UP FANTASY KINGDOM CHANNELING HIGH CONTRAST BETWEEN MISERY AND ECSTASY.

I SAW A BALD GIRL.

SHE WAS BALD, EXCEPT WITH A LITTLE TUFT OF HAIR OVER HER FOREHEAD. MAYBE SHE SHAVED IT ALL OFF FOR THE SAKE OF SOME KIND OF **ALTERNATIVE VISIBILITY**? WAS IT SUBCULTURAL VISIBILITY? GAY VISIBILITY? BOTH? I HAD NEVER SEEN A BALD GIRL IN MY ENTIRE LIFE. **EXCEPT SUSAN POWTER ON TELEVISION** AND WHILE I DEFINITELY LOVED SUSAN......

THIS WAS TOTALLY DIFFERENT. I WAS HAVING A DIFFICULT TIME DIFFERENTIATING BETWEEN HOW MUCH I WANTED TO BE THIS **BOYISH FIGURE** WHO CARRIED EONS OF **HOMO-EROTIC POWER**; AND HOW MUCH I SUDDENLY JUST WANTED TO **DATE THEM**.... HOLD THEIR HAND AS WE ESCAPED THE DARK, DAMP CLOSET WHERE MY SKELETONS SLEPT.

THE BALD GIRL'S EYES STOPPED TIME AS THEY MOVED BETWEEN HARSH FLUORESCENTS AND THE SEA-FOAM GREEN BODY OF WATER SURROUNDING HER PUPILS. THEY STOPPED TIME, AS I FINALLY FELT WHAT REAL INFATUATION WAS LIKE, AND "GOING TO PASALAQUA" BY GREEN DAY LOOPED REPEATEDLY IN MY MIND. BALD GIRL'S FACE LEFT ME SHOCKED AND FRAZZLED. AND SHE WASN'T JUST THERE, KEEPING TO HERSELF, TWIDDLING HER FINGERS AND UNDERMINING MY EXISTENCE. SHE WAS LOOKING AT ME.

I REPLAYED THE EXPERIENCE OVER AND OVER IN MY HEAD, LOCKING THE INEVITABLE PATH BETWEEN THE BALD GIRL'S FACE AND MINE, PUNCHING IN MY NAME, BIRTH DATE, AND BLOOD TYPE IN THE BANK OF HER SUBCONSCIOUS. MAYBE SHE WILL THINK ABOUT ME TOMORROW? I THOUGHT TO MYSELF, HALF-DISMAL, HALF-ELATED.

I WAS ON A FOURTH-DIMENSIONAL STROLL THROUGH THE FUTURE. I DIDN'T CARE IF ALEX EVEN LIKED GREEN DAY. SHE WAS BALD. IT WAS RELIEVING AND HUMANIZING TO HAVE LEGITIMATE FEELINGS FOR A LIVING PERSON WHO I COULD EXPECT TO RUN INTO ON ANY OLD DAY.

I USUALLY FELT LIKE I WAS FLOATING IN AN UNCHARTED SPACE WHERE MY FEELINGS WERE HAZARDOUS, SO MY SELF-ASSURANCE FLAILED WITH THE WIND. BUT I WAS LOUD IN NATURE, INTERESTED IN QUESTIONING EVERYONE'S EVERY GESTURE, AND HAPPY TO BE OUTLANDISH– SO I COULD EASILY FOOL EVERYONE WHILE I LAUGHED AT EVERYTHING. STILL, I DON'T THINK ANY OF MY FRIENDS COULD YET SEE THE FIRE THAT SURROUNDED ME.

CLARITA SEEMED GENERALLY AMUSED AND INTERESTED IN THE THINGS I HAD TO SAY, AND I COULD LISTEN TO HER ALL DAY IN RETURN. SHE MADE ME FEEL *NORMAL*; LIKE GREEN DAY DID. AS IF IN SOME OTHER DIMENSION I COULD EXIST AND HAVE AN OPENLY QUESTIONABLE SEXUALITY AND IT'S NOT A BIG DEAL . . . AND IF THAT IDENTITY IS EVER THREATENED, I COULD ROLL MY EYES OR FART BECAUSE *WHO FUCKING CARED* — I EXISTED, INDEPENDENTLY AND CON-SCIOUSLY, SOMEPLACE ELSE. I WANTED TO STAY IN THAT PLACE WHERE THE PEOPLE WHO GAVE ME SHIT DIDN'T MATTER, AND THE PEOPLE WHO MATTERED FELT CONFOUNDED TOO. SOMETIMES, EVERYTHING SEEMED LIKE IT WAS GOING TO BE ALL RIGHT — EVERY TIME I TALKED TO CLARITA ABOUT THE FUTURE, AND EVERY TIME I LISTENED TO GREEN DAY.

CHAPTER FIVE

ONE OF MY LIES

"SO THIS IS GONNA BE MY LIFE," I THOUGHT RIDING HOME FROM SCHOOL ON THE LAST DAY BEFORE WINTER BREAK. SETTING THE PAST ASIDE, I COULD FINALLY SAY "FUCK IT," BUT ONLY WHEN I WASN'T DEPRESSED OR UNHAPPY ABOUT THE WAY I LOOK, OR ABOUT THE WAY THAT I CAN'T BE OUT TO ANYBODY, BECAUSE IT MIGHT EXCOMMUNICATE ME FROM MY CUBAN-AMERICA.

MAMA HAD A SMIRK, WHICH FORMED EVERY TIME I TALKED ABOUT GREEN DAY.

SHE LIKED MY SELF-ASSURANCE, LOOMING BEHIND THE HAZE OF GREEN DAY AND SELF. AT TIMES LIKE THESE, I PLACED SOCIALIZA-TION AND CATHOLICISM ON THE CURB...

... AND LEFT THEM WAITING FOR THE NEXT PICKUP TRUCK ON ITS WAY TO NAZARETH.

AT TIMES LIKE THESE, I COULD FEEL HALF-SANE AND RIGHTEOUSLY AWARE OF THE VALUES MY FAMILY AND I COULD HOLD ONTO TOGETHER, AS WORKING WOMEN AT ODDS WITH THE CLASS STRUCTURE OF MIAMI.

PLUS, I WAS OUT TO GREEN DAY. I TOLD THEM IN A LETTER ONCE. SO I BASICALLY WAS OUT TO EVERYONE BY TELEPATHIC TRANSITIVE PROPERTY. I WAS HAPPY TO PLACE ALL THAT INVISIBLE WEIGHT ON GREEN DAY'S HYPOTHETICAL SHOULDERS.

CRISTY'S BAGGAGE 1982-1994

WHEN I GOT BACK HOME I GOT TO THINKING ABOUT "THE AGE OF AQUARIUS." THIS KID, FRANK, REFERENCED IT ONCE. I ALWAYS WANTED TO KNOW WHAT IT WAS. IT WAS MINE AND FIFI'S FRIENDSHIP SONG, GODDAMMIT. AND THROUGH OUR ENTIRE EXPERIENCE, I DID NOT KNOW WHAT THE HELL MARILYN MCCOO WAS COOING ABOUT — SO BEAUTIFULLY, TO THE POINT WHERE WE RECORDED THE SONG BACK TO BACK SO WE COULD ALWAYS HEAR IT TWICE. PLUS, I REALLY BELIEVED IN ASTROLOGY, DEEPLY AND SERIOUSLY.

FRANK TOLD ME THAT WAS BECAUSE I WAS PROBABLY A DYKE. HE DID NOT SAY IT IN A POSITIVE WAY, BUT THAT'S BESIDE THE POINT.

HE CLAIMED TO BE SATANIC, AND HE CLAIMED TO HAVE SEEN THE DEVIL ONCE, WHICH EXPLAINED HIS INTEREST IN DUBBING STRUCTURED RELIGION A SHAM. WE CLASHED QUITE OFTEN, BECAUSE HE WAS A DIFFERENT KIND OF ANGRY, BUT HE WAS RANTING ONE DAY ABOUT THE "AGES," SO I LISTENED.

BASICALLY, THE AQUARIUS WATER BEARER APPEARS AT THE END OF THE BIBLE, IN AN EXCHANGE WITH JESUS CHRIST, WHERE THEY PASS ALONG THE TORCH TO THE NEXT MESSIAH. EXPECTANTLY, THE WATER BEARER CARRIES KNOWLEDGE OF CHRIST'S IDEOLOGICAL MISTAKES. THIS EXCHANGE IS THE CATALYST FOR THE NEXT AGE.

EVERY AGE LASTS ABOUT 2150 YEARS, AND JESUS WAS THE MESSIAH PAINTED FOR THE CURRENT AGE WE'RE IN — THE AGE OF PISCES.

...I'M NOT REALLY INTO ASTROLOGY THOUGH, THAT STUFF IS HOKEY.

SO BASICALLY, AT THE END OF THE AGE OF PISCES, JESUS AS MESSIAH WILL COME TO AN END, AND THE AGE OF AQUARIUS WILL SUPPOSEDLY BEGIN . . . EVERY REPRODUCTION OF THE BIBLE SINCE *HELL-KNOWS-WHEN* HAS REWRITTEN THIS ENDING . . . I GUESS BECAUSE NOBODY WANTED TO TELL THE WORLD THAT IN THE AGE OF AQUARIUS, ALL OF THE PRIESTS AND POPES ARE GOING TO BURN AND THE DEVIL WILL COME . . . *BWAHAHAHA.*

I DID NOT BELIEVE THE DEVIL WOULD COME BECAUSE AQUARIUS, THE WATER BEARER, WAS AN AIR SIGN, LIKE ME. COMMUNICATION AND SOCIAL HARMONY WAS OUR DEEP, LONGED-FOR DESIRE WHETHER OR NOT WE KNEW HOW TO ACHIEVE IT. AND THE DEVIL REPRESENTS NONCONSENSUAL BONDAGE, WHICH IS SOMETHING THIS "AQUARIAN AGE" COULD NEVER REPRESENT. ESPECIALLY WHEN COMPARED WITH "THE AGE OF AQUARIUS" BY THE 5TH DIMENSION.

HE KEPT INSISTING THE RAM HORNS, DURING THE PREVIOUS AGE OF ARIES, WERE ADDITIONALLY REMINISCENT OF THE DEVIL, THUS AN OPPOSITION TO THE AGE OF JESUS, BECAUSE FRANK WAS A SATANIC SEPERATIST WHO WAS OKAY WITH LYING IN ORDER TO PROVE HIS POINT. RAM HORNS CLEARLY HAVE *NOTHING* TO DO WITH THE DEVIL BECAUSE THERE IS NO MENACING DEVIL IF THERE IS NO TOTALITARIAN GOD — JUST UNIVERSAL SPIRITUALITY. I HAD BEEN RESEARCHING THIS FOR YEARS IN HORTY'S SET OF *WORLD BOOK ENCYCLOPEDIAS*, AND HAD NOT FOUND A DEEP DISCOURSE BEYOND FRANK'S DIALOGUE. BUT BASICALLY, THE END OF DAYS DOESN'T MEAN THE END OF THE WORLD BUT THE END OF THE AGE OF *THE CHRISTIAN RIGHT:*

THE AGE OF FEAR AND FANATICAL MARTYRDOM. THE DAWNING OF THE AGE OF AQUARIUS STARTED WITH CIVIL RIGHTS, AS THE 5TH DIMENSION TOLD US.

I BELIEVED IN COLLECTIVE CONSCIOUSNESS AND THE FACT THAT I WAS NOT ALONE, AS THE MEDIA SLOWLY EXPOSED MY ALTERNATIVE VALUES. THIS MADE MY CLOSET FEEL SAFE . . . JUST ME, GREEN DAY, EQUAL RIGHTS INFOMERCIALS, AND MY CONVICTIONS. I FELT BETTER ABOUT CONSCIOUSNESS-SHIFTING, THE POSSIBILITIES OF THE FUTURE, AND MY APATHY WITH THE PRESENT . . .

BECAUSE I KNEW MY FAMILY DID THEIR ULTIMATE BEST AS WOMEN IN A WORLD OF MEN, WORKING HARD TO SUPPORT CHILDREN, AND PUTTING THEIR RESERVATIONS ASIDE IN ORDER TO SEE US HAPPY. STILL, I DID NOT UNDERSTAND SOME PEOPLE'S HOGGING OF RELIGIOUS VALUES BASED ON A BOOK WRITTEN A LONG TIME AGO, WHICH UNDERSTANDABLY HAS BEEN USED AS A TOOL TO CONSTRUCT CULTURE AND CREATE PEACE, BUT ALSO TO JUSTIFY HATE— AND WHAT IS THE POINT IN BELIEVING IN SOMETHING IF IT'S LYING ABOUT THE WAY THINGS JUST ARE?

I THOUGHT ALL THIS WOULD SEND ME TO HELL UNTIL BILLIE JOE RATIONALIZED MY FOUNDATION. WHO WOULD HAVE THOUGHT THE PHILOSOPHY ARTICULATED BY A 21-YEAR-OLD HIGH SCHOOL DROPOUT WOULD MOVE THIS MOUNTAIN CALLED SELF-HATE? I HAD NO IDEA, BUT IT MADE COMPLETE SENSE. BECAUSE IF YOU'RE ABLE TO QUESTION YOUR SEXUALITY AND RELIGION, ARTICULATE ANGER, AND JUSTIFY YOUR MEANS, YOU'RE PROBABLY DOING ALL RIGHT. I WAS STARTING TO ENJOY MY IDENTITY . . .

. . AS OPPOSED TO JUST LEARNING HOW TO TRANSLATE IT TO A WORLD THAT DID NOT WANT O LISTEN. I SAW NO REASON FOR GOING TO HELL AND BEING ENSLAVED BY THAT KID *FRANK* ND HIS SATANIC FRIENDS. I DID NOT WISH I WAS STRAIGHT; I JUST WISHED EVERYONE ELSE OULD BEGIN TO ACCEPT ME, RATHER THAN *TOLERATE* ME, LIKE YOU WOULD A DRIPPING FAUCET R A WASPS' NEST FORMING OUTSIDE THE KITCHEN WINDOW.
. . THIS WHOLE "I'M LONELY/I'M GAY" THING WAS BEGINNING TO MAKE A LOT OF SENSE, NOW THAT ILLIE JOE HAD WRITTEN THESE SONGS THAT COULD ASSIST ME IN UNCOVERING EVERY BIT AND IECE OF MYSELF.

I DECIDED TO BECOME ACQUAINTED WITH THE SKELETONS IN MY CLOSET, NOW THAT I WOULD SPEND TWO WEEKS AWAY FROM THE REST OF THE WORLD. THE SKELETONS WOULD COMFORT ME AT NIGHT, BECAUSE I KNEW THAT THE TRUTH MIGHT MAKE PEOPLE ANGRY, DISTURBED, OR CONFUSED. AND I THOUGHT I COULD JUST HIDE SOMEWHERE — UNTIL THE TRUTH FELT SAFE.

THE AGE OF AQUARIUS MIGHT SIGNIFY AN ERA OF HUMANITY UNDERSTANDING THE FALSENESS OF STRUCTURED RELIGION. THE SUN AND STARS AND TREES WOULD BECOME THEORETICAL GODS, AND RELIGION WOULD BE DISMISSED IF IT STANDS FOR ANYTHING BUT HARMONY, UNDERSTANDING, AND FORGIVENESS — JUST LIKE THE QUALITIES OF THOSE BORN UNDER THE CONSTELLATION OF AQUARIUS.

BILLIE JOE ARMSTRONG IS AN *AQUARIUS*.

SO, TELL ME ABOUT *YOUR* NEEDS?

ASTROLOGY WAS OBVIOUS, LIKE ENVIRONMENTAL SCIENCE. WHEN THE PLANETS ARE HERE AND THE SUN IS HERE, THINGS THAT GROW ARE LIKE THIS . . . DUH. VERY OBVIOUS AND EASY TO UNDERSTAND, ESPECIALLY IF YOURE A DYKE; SO I'VE HEARD.

I LISTENED TO GREEN DAY BECAUSE THEY MADE ME FEEL ALIVE, LIKE AEROSMITH AND BROADWAY MUSICALS DO. SOMETIMES, BEING ALIVE FELT DROLL, UNTIL I THOUGHT ABOUT THE FUTURE. BECAUSE I WAS AWARE THAT THERE EXISTS A RADICAL QUEER WORLD WHICH, FOR NOW, FELT AS FAR AWAY AS 3-AND-A-HALF DAYS ON A GREYHOUND BUS FROM MIAMI, FL TO BERKELEY, CA.

FOR NOW, AS MY PUNK ASPIRATIONS HAD SETTLED INTO A PATIENT SPACE, ALL I COULD THINK OF WAS MY EVER-CHANGING BODY, MY HAIR, AND WHAT WOULD HAPPEN IF I COULD I CUT IT ALL OFF. I WORE MY BRAID LIKE A BUTCH MEDAL OF HONOR. MY COUSIN, GABRIEL, HAD ASSUMED I WAS BORN WITH IT GROWING OUT OF MY HEAD. IN SECRECY, THE ATTENTION TO MY DAILY APPEARANCE FILTERED INTO DAILY BIOLOGICAL QUIRKS.

I WAS A HAPLESS HORMONE. I WOULD DAYDREAM ABOUT **ASSHOLES,** **LACTATING BREASTS,** AND THE **VAGINAL SHAPES THAT APPEARED IN NATURE** AS MUCH AS I DAYDREAMED OF ALEX, AND AS MUCH AS I PLAYED GREEN DAY ON **REPEAT.**

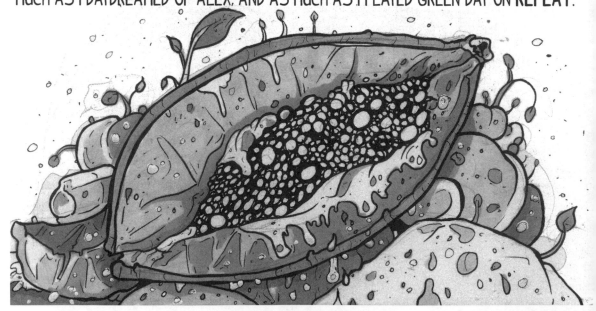

SEXUALIZED EVERYTHING
[T]HAT RESEMBLED ANYTHING
[B]ODILY. I DID NOT KNOW HOW TO
[C]ONCEAL THIS, AND AS A GEMINI,
[I]T WAS DIFFICULT TO JUST NOT
[S]HARE SOMETHING.

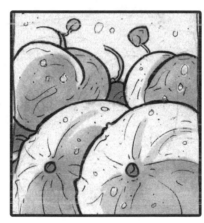

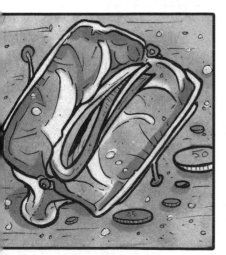

SO I BORE THE
CLAUSTROPHOBIA AND
LAUGHED TO MYSELF
EVERY TIME SOMEONE
PULLED A COOKIE OUT
OF THE COOKIE JAR.
EVERY TIME SOMEONE
PULLED A QUARTER OUT
OF THEIR POCKET.
**EVERY TIME I
HEARD THE WORD
"LIP," I DIED INSIDE.**

SOMETIMES I HID IN THE BATHROOM. I WOULD STARE FOR HOURS AT THE IRREGULARITIES OF MY BODY, AND IMAGINED THE DAY WHERE ASYMMETRICAL BREASTS WOULD BE ADORED.

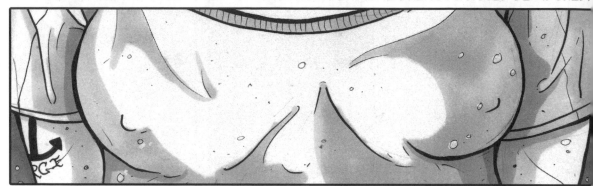

I WOULD COUNT THE NEW HAIRS UNDER MY ARMPITS LIKE THEY WERE DOLLAR BILLS FLYING OUT OF THE LIME TREE.

I IMAGINED ALEX -- IRREGULAR, BEAUTIFUL, AND IN THE SAME ROOM AS ME. DRINKING COFFEE LISTENING TO RECORDS, EATING EACH OTHER OUT, AND WATCHING THE SUNSET, DURING OUR IMAGINARY ADULT LIFE. I IMAGINED A FUTURE BASED IN A VORTEX, WHERE REALITY WAS *SUSPENDED* AND LOVE AT FIRST SIGHT FILTERED INTO OUR ADULT EXPERIENCES.

MY IMAGINATION WAS ALL I HAD ON THESE ISOLATED TUESDAYS AFTER I REALIZED THAT ALEX WAS ALMOST THREE YEARS OLDER THAN ME, THUS TOTALLY UNATTAINABLE.

ALEX WAS A NOTORIOUSLY CELEBRATED CLASS CLOWN. THE OTHER KIDS TALKED ABOUT ALEX LIKE SHE WAS *EROTICA*-ERA MADONNA. BUT FOR MY OWN SAKE, I WOULD ENTERTAIN ALEX'S POTENTIAL INSECURITIES AND CREATE AN IMAGINARY MIDDLE GROUND BETWEEN US . . .

SO, I WONDERED IF ALEX WAS AS TORTURED AS THE REST OF US, WHO REPRESENTED REBELLION ON THE OUTSIDE, BUT TOILED DEEPLY ON THE INSIDE?

AS I HID IN MY TORTURED COCOON THAT DAY, I CHOSE TO ESCAPE REALITY THROUGH THE GAYEST OF DANCE POP AND AN ORGASM. I PUT "VOGUE" ON MY WALKMAN AND EMBRACED MY WOMANHOOD. MADONNA KNEW WHAT I WAS GOING THROUGH, YOU KNOW? THE DISCONNECT FROM A WORLD THAT ISN'T READY FOR OUR FIRE . . . SO I HID AWAY IN THE ONE PLACE WHERE I COULD BE GAY AND IN LOVE AND FULFILLED, WITHOUT THE FEAR OF APPALLING ANYBODY AND WITHOUT THE TORTURE THAT CAME WITH HAVING A CRUSH. I HID IN MY BATHROOM AND TRIED TO WATER DOWN THE ANXIETY THAT CAME WITH DAILY LIFE IN THE CLOSET. AND TO TOP THAT OFF, APPARENTLY I MISSED GREEN DAY ON *SATURDAY NIGHT LIVE*. AND YOU KNOW WHO WAS THE HOST? ROSEANNE BARR. I MISSED IT, AND WILL BE WAITING ON BENDED KNEE NEXT TO MY *TV GUIDE* UNTIL IT RE-AIRS.

IT WAS JUST ONE OF THOSE DAYS WHERE SEX AND LOVE FELT ISOLATING AND DIFFICULT. NECESSARY -- BUT DIFFICULT.

I WAITED PATIENTLY FOR THE DAY TO END.

THE VISIBLE SURFACE OF GREEN DAY WAS BROKEN DOWN INTO VULNERABLE EXPERIENCES, CHIPPED TEETH, MAKESHIFT CLOTHING, AND SHAPE-SHIFT HAIR. THEY WERE NOT DRESSED, PACKAGED, OR DONE-UP FOR THE CAMERA (ALTHOUGH THEY WERE APPARENTLY SELLOUTS TO A VAST PORTION OF THE PUNK ROCK COMMUNITY). UNDERSTANDING THAT HUMANKIND GETS OLD AND RESPONSIBLE, I MADE MY OWN DEFINITION OF SELLING OUT. I KNEW IT WAS GETTING TIRED FAST WITHOUT CONSIDERATION FOR YOUR BELIEFS. I THOUGHT IF ONE WAS OFFERED FINANCIAL STABILITY AND THE OPTION TO STAY TRUE TO THEIR IDENTITY, HOW MUCH FINANCIAL CUSHION AND/OR SERIOUS PUNK ROCK DEVOTION DOES SOMEONE NEED TO HAVE IN ORDER TO SAY NO?

BECAUSE, FRANKLY, THE CLASS WAR WAS EXHAUSTING, AND I WAS TIRED OF FIGHTING IT.

I WAS NOT AFRAID OF JUSTIFYING GREEN DAY'S PLACE IN POPULAR CULTURE, WHICH HAS BOTH DEFACED THEIR TRUE UPBRINGING *AND* BROUGHT THEM TO MY TELEVISION SET. BECAUSE I KNEW THAT POPULAR CULTURE WAS MOSTLY WHAT WAS ACCESSIBLE TO US . . . US PEOPLE SURVIVING IN COMMUNITIES THAT AREN'T THE HIGHLY ALTERNATIVE, HIGHLY METROPOLITAN VORTEXES OF BIG CITIES WITH BIG ALTERNATIVE VALUES. US PEOPLE LIVING IN CULTURES THAT REJECT PROGRESSIVE-AMERICAN VALUES FOR THE SAKE OF CREATING THE SOLID FOUNDATION OF *UNA FAMILIA CUBANA.* I BELIEVED THAT GREEN DAY WAS IN FACT NOT THE FLASHY BULLSHIT POPULAR CULTURE REPRESENTED, WHETHER OR NOT THEY GOT RICH.

GREEN DAY CAME FROM THE SAME PLACE A BUNCH OF OTHER ECONOMICALLY DISENFRANCHISED PEOPLE CAME FROM. THE PROSPECT OF FINANCIAL STABILITY IS ALWAYS AN EXCUSE TO GIVE EVERYTHING UP, BECAUSE FRANKLY IT SUCKS TO BE BROKE, AND IT TAKES SOMETHING BETWEEN A FAT WALLET AND EXTREME FAMILIAL SOLACE TO DENY THIS.

IN THE END, ACCORDING TO ALL THE BOOKS AND NEWSPAPERS, GREEN DAY LOST ALL PUNK CREDIBILITY. THEY COULD NEVER GO BACK TO 924 GILMAN ST., THE CLUB THEIR SCENE WAS BUILT AROUND, *EVER AGAIN*. FOR SOME REASON, IT HURT ME, AS IF I COULD NOT GO BACK THERE MYSELF, AS IF I WAS THE ONE WHO HAD LOST THAT PRECIOUS COMMUNITY WHICH WAS MANIFESTED THROUGH AN AUDIO BLEND OF THE ME-LODIC AND GRUFF, XEROXED PALETTES OF THE MOST BEAUTIFUL ART I HAD EVER SEEN, AND RAMPANT GAY VISIBILITY. I HAD DEEP-SEATED ANXIETY ON THEIR BEHALF, AND IF I COULD GO BACK AND DO IT ALL AGAIN, WITHOUT LOSING THE COMMUNITY, WITHOUT COMPROMISING, I PROBABLY WOULD.

I CHANNELED THIS AS IF IT COULD BE ME — LOSING THE CUBAN COMMUNITY, WHICH HARVESTED MY IDENTITY — IN ORDER TO FULFILL A PROPHECY OF SURVIVING SOMEDAY.

I EXPLORED MY SURROUNDINGS EXCEEDING MY USUAL BOUNDARIES, CALLING RADIO STATIONS AND ASKING QUESTIONS. EVENTUALLY, I LEARNED THE MASS MEDIA WAS MOSTLY CHRONICLING MILES OF RE-REGURGITATED PRESS RELEASES, COMPILED FROM THE REMAINS OF SOME LINEAR MOTIF SOMEONE WITH A PART-TIME JOB AT WARNER BROS. PULLED OUT OF THEIR ASSHOLE. THE TRUTH WAS SNIPPED OUT, LIKE THE RECONSTRUCTED BIBLE.

GREEN DAY, IN FACT, HAD THIS REAL PAST AND THIS REAL LEGACY WITH TANGENTS UPON TANGENTS OF CREATIVE REVOLUTIONS AND *QUEER* ACCEPTANCE, ACCORDING TO THE ONE SOURCE I DID TRUST, A VIDEOTAPED INTERVIEW WITH JON GINOLI FROM PANSY DIVISION.

THE PRECIOUS CREATIONS I WAS SLOWLY UNVEILING, AS I
LEARNED ABOUT MY FAMILY AND MY NEWFANGLED NEEDS, WERE
REMINISCENT OF THE THINGS MIMITA FOUND IN CATHOLIC CULTURE,
WHICH SHE USED TO SUSTAIN HER OWN FAMILY. HER SPIRITUAL LEANINGS
SOUGHT AFTER THAT HARMONY AND UNDERSTANDING, DESPITE THE
FLAWED TEACHINGS THAT CAME WITH ANY 20TH-CENTURY BIBLE STUDY.

MY FINDINGS WERE THE SAME: HONEST AND DECORATIVE, WITH AN
INTEREST IN PROVIDING A SHOULDER TO THOSE WITH LESS TO LEAN ON.
A TOKEN OF SALVATION, BUT CONSTRUCTED FOR THE
BIOLOGICAL SHIFTS AND SPIRITUAL SPLITS OF
MY QUEER GENERATION.

SCHOOL WAS IN SESSION AGAIN. THE DAY STARTED WITH AN UNBEARABLE REACTION TO A RUMOR ABOUT SOME KID'S ASSUMED GAY IDENTITY. THE REACTION PAINED ME, BUT THE RUMOR MADE MY SKIN HOT, BOTHERED, AND *ALIVE*. LIKE HERE IS A SUGGESTION OF ADULTHOOD, *THIS IS WHAT SHARING SPACE WITH OTHER HOMOS FEELS LIKE!* EXCITING YET ISOLATING. I FOR ONE NEEDED THE CONVOLUTED RELEASE. MY BRAIN AND HEART WERE A MESS. I SERIOUSLY THOUGHT ABOUT ALEX EVERY NIGHT, ALL VACATION LONG, MOURNING THE LARGE POSSIBILITY THAT SHE WOULD NEVER LOOK AT ME, EVER AGAIN, FOR THE REST OF MY LIFE.

BULL. SHIT.

HEARTBREAK WAS A STRANGE NEW FEELING. CLASPED BETWEEN MY HEART AND STOMACH, I COULD FEEL EXPLODING VOMIT, TWIRLING GROWTHS, AND INSECTS. I HAD NOT GENUINELY FELT IT YET, UNTIL NOW . . .

. . . AS I FOUND MYSELF ENAMORED BY A FACE THAT MOST LIKELY FELT NOTHING FOR ME. UNREQUITED LOVE WAS NATURALLY ADOLESCENT, SO WHY BOTHER TRYING TO CHANGE IT? UNTIL I SAW HER AGAIN, I DID NOT MIND FEELING A BIT PATHETIC, BECAUSE FOR THE FIRST TIME, I ACTUALLY *LIKED* SOMEONE.

I LIKED SOMEONE. LIKE THE GIRLS WHO WROTE "I HEART SO AND SO" ON EVERY ONE OF THEIR FOLDERS. I WAS OFFICIALLY A TEENAGER WITH HORMONES DEARLY DEVOTED TO A PEER RATHER THAN A CULTURAL ICON. BUT I COULDN'T TELL ANYONE BESIDES THE BATHROOM STALL.

I COULDN'T TALK ABOUT ALEX TO ANYONE, SO I TALKED ABOUT GREEN DAY INSTEAD, AS WELL AS DETAILS ON MY OCCASIONAL CRUSH ON NAMELESS-TORTURED-GRUNGE-GUY-OF-THE-WEEK. I GUESS I DID NOT KNOW HOW TO TALK MUCH ABOUT ANYTHING BESIDES GREEN DAY. MARIMAR WAS THE FIRST HUMAN IN EXISTENCE TO COMMENT ON THIS, SO I ASSESSED IT. I ADMIRED MARIMAR AND THE WAY HER ADVICE ALWAYS FELT RIGHT. HER APPROVAL OR MUTUAL ADMIRATION FELT LIKE A GREEN LIGHT FOR PRE-TEEN HAVOC — CHAOS-FREE. SO I CONSIDERED WALKING ON EGGSHELLS AND PRACTICED THE COMPLICATED ART OF *NOT TALKING ABOUT GREEN DAY.* I WOULD OFTEN FAIL.

I'M GUESSING IT WAS MY PERIOD? BUT I HAD A NEWFOUND HORMONAL IMBALANCE WHICH LED ME TO CONSIDER EVERY MEMBER OF GREEN DAY, THE ONLY CUTE BOYS TO TRULY EXIST ON THIS EARTH. MARIMAR COULD UNDERSTAND. SHE CARRIED A SINCERE DEVOTION TO SENSITIVE ARTISTS WITH PENCHANTS FOR FEELINGS LIKE JEFF BUCKLEY AND THE CRANBERRIES. SHE COULD SEE THE FINE LINE BETWEEN ART AND LOVE. I COULD BE HEAD OVER HEELS IN LOVE WITH BILLIE JOE ARMSTRONG, AND IT COULD BE CELEBRATED, DESPITE THE OCCASIONAL GUILT ONE MIGHT FEEL WHEN PARADING AROUND THEIR SEXUAL ATTRACTION TO THEIR ROLE MODEL. DESPITE THE OCCASIONAL SELF-LOATHING, AT THE END OF THE DAY, I JUST WANTED TO HOLD ALEX. I WANTED TO RUB HER HEAD WITH BOTH MY HANDS AND KISS HER AND STARE AT HER AND KISS HER AGAIN. BUT THE ONLY TIME I WAS ABLE TO DO THIS WAS IN MY DREAMS.

I COULD HAVE VERY WELL COME OUT TO MARIMAR AND CLARITA. I COULD HAVE. BUT I WAS 13 YEARS OLD. AND IF THAT WASN'T A GOOD EXCUSE FOR FEELING TERRIFIED, WHAT WAS?

I WOULD ALWAYS LISTEN TO "COMING CLEAN" ON REPEAT. I LEARNED HOW TO USE THE REPEAT FUNCTION ON MY CD PLAYER SO I WOULDN'T HAVE TO SUSPICIOUSLY CREEP INTO MY BAG TO CHANGE THE SONG. CHACHI THOUGHT THIS WAS FUNNY, AND I QUESTIONED MY SKEPTICISM OF MEN EVERY TIME I WAS WITH HIM. WE HAD ART CLASS TOGETHER, AND OUR ANGST-RIDDEN CONNECTION ALLOWED US TO SHARE EVERYTHING. IN A FLANNEL SHIRT HE LOOKED LIKE A YOUNG STEVEN TYLER WHO DIDN'T EAT MUCH AND ROLLED IN THE DIRT. CHACHI TOOK ME SERIOUSLY. HE MADE ME FEEL LIKE ONE OF THE GUYS, IN THE MOST SELF-REWARDING WAY POSSIBLE.

I MADE THOSE SAME OLD MASTURBATION JOKES, AND CHACHI LAUGHED. THEN HE ASKED ME WHERE THE JOKE ORIGINATED AND CONTINUED TO ASK ME ABOUT MY FAVORITE SONG OFF *TOYS IN THE ATTIC* BY AEROSMITH.

CHACHI WAS ALWAYS CARVING LETTERS INTO HIS SKIN. I WAS ALWAYS MAKING SARCASTIC SELF-DEPRECATING JOKES. WE KNEW THAT THERE WAS MORE TO LIFE. BUT FOR NOW WE NEEDED TO BASK IN THE PAIN THAT WASN'T READY TO GO AWAY. OUR TEACHER WAS AN INCREDIBLE HIGH SPIRIT NAMED MS. GARCIA. SHE LET ME IMPLEMENT *REN & STIMPY* OR GREEN DAY IN EVERY SINGLE ONE OF MY ASSIGNMENTS. I DIDN'T HAVE MS. NAVARRO THIS SEMESTER, BUT I HAD MS. GARCIA AND CHACHI, HOVERING AROUND ME, MAKING ME FEEL CLOSER TO SANE.

WE SAT TOGETHER, FUCKING UP AND WONDERING WHERE WE WOULD GO NEXT, AND WHAT OUR MOTHERS WOULD THINK IF THEY EVER FOUND OUT THAT THERE WERE THINGS ABOUT US THAT MIGHT GENUINELY FRIGHTEN THEM.

WHEN I LEFT CLASS THAT DAY IN FEBRUARY, CHACHI KISSED ME ON THE CHEEK. I DID NOT KNOW WHAT IT DID TO MY VAGINA, BUT IT DID SOMETHING THAT MADE ME FEEL *BISEXUAL* (AS LONG AS HE STILL SAW ME AS ONE OF THE GUYS). BUT THE SENSATION DISSIPATED. HUMAN TOUCH IS SURREAL, AND IT TOOK A FEW SECONDS TO REGISTER IF THE KISS WAS FLIRTATIOUS OR JUST THE TRADITONAL CUBAN "HELLO." AND FOR SOME REASON, I DIDN'T CARE. I WANTED CHACHI TO BE ONE OF MY BEST FRIENDS. SO, I WONDERED IF MY BODY WAS PUSHING THE SUBTLE ATTRACTIONS TOWARD BOYS BECAUSE IT KNEW THE TRUE DIFFICULTY BEHIND MY ATTRACTIONS TOWARD ANYONE ELSE, UNREQUITED OR NOT.

I STOOD OUTSIDE AND WAITED FOR MY AUNT. THE SUN WAS CRIPPLING AND I LOOKED AROUND FOR SOMETHING TO COOL ME OFF. INSTEAD, I BROKE OUT INTO A SWEAT.

ALEX PASSED RIGHT BY ME.

SHE TURNED TOWARD ME, BUT COULD VERY WELL HAVE BEEN LOOKING AT THE KID BEHIND ME.

OH MY GOD, I THINK SHE SMILED.

MY STOMACH CHURNED AND I WANTED TO PUKE, BUT MY VAGINA PUKED INSTEAD, MUCH MORE SO THAN WHEN CHACHI KISSED ME ON THE CHEEK. ALEX'S MERE GLANCE SPARKLED, AND I FELT A LITTLE LOST AND CONFOUNDED. BUT I LEARNED THAT I WAS, IN FACT, NOT STRAIGHT, SO I DID NOT HAVE TO WONDER ANYMORE IF ANYTHING WAS GOING TO CHANGE. I'M HORMONALLY FLUID, BUT ENTIRELY QUEER. IT WAS UPLIFTING BUT FRIGHTENING, BECAUSE NOW I HAD TO LOVE MY IDENTITY, WHETHER OR NOT ANYONE WOULD EVER UNDERSTAND.

ESPERANZA ARRIVED AND I CRAWLED INTO HER CAR. WE HAD A SIMILAR INTEREST IN GIRLTALK AND FRIVOLOUS EMOTIONAL BANTER SO I GOT TO TALK ABOUT MY DAY THROUGH A FAMILY-FRIENDLY FILTER.

OYE, ISN'T BILLIE JOE *CUTE*?

YEAH HE'S CUTE! AY, IS THAT THE KIND OF GUY YOU LIKE?! YOU WOULD HAVE **LOVED** ALL THE **ITALIAN BOYS** I USED TO SEE AROUND WHEN I LIVED IN **NEW JERSEY**.

AYYYY! YOU HAVE TO UNDERSTAND THAT I DONT LIKE GREEN DAY BECAUSE THEY ARE CUTE. THEIR MUSIC AND LYRICS, LIKE, CHANGED MY LIFE. OKAY?

YES HONEY, I KNOW YOU LIKE THEIR MUSIC. AY, I CAN'T WAIT TO TELL YOUR MOM!

GOD, WHY DID I EVEN SAY ANYTHING, I'M SUCH A GEMINI.

I GUESS I WAS A *WOMAN* WITH *HORMONES* FOR THE FIRST TIME -- TO MY FAMILY, AT LEAST -- WHICH PRESENTED A FRIGHTENING MOMENT.
I KNEW NOW THAT MY BUTCH AESTHETIC WAS A KID'S AESTHETIC IN THE EYES OF MOST ADULTS. A GIRL'S NEED TO PRESENT LIKE A BOY WAS TOO OFTEN DISMISSED AS A PHASE.
BEING ACCEPTED AS A TOMBOY FELT LIKE A CONCEPT THAT COULD ONLY LAST FOR SO LONG. I WAS TURNING 13 YEARS OLD THAT YEAR. SO *THEN* WHAT HAPPENS?

I SPENT THE NEXT FEW WEEKS

REALIZING THAT I WAS READY TO GIVE UP ON MY DAYDREAMS OF POTENTIAL LIFE PURSUITS WHICH I HAD HELD ONTO FOR THE LAST FEW YEARS. THE STAND-UP COMEDIAN, THE BROADWAY STAR, THE FEMINIST ASTRONAUT, THE VETERINARIAN WHO MADE HOUSE CALLS, AND DID I SAY *THE STAND-UP COMEDIAN?* -- THAT ONE WAS THE MOST DIFFICULT ONE TO DUST OFF. I SPENT TWO LONG YEARS IMPERSONATING JERRY SEINFELD AND WEARING BRIGHT WHITE REEBOK SNEAKERS TO FURTHER GET INTO CHARACTER, ONLY TO REALIZE I COULD NOT CREATE MY OWN VERSION OF HIM. I HAD FOUND THIS BETTER VERSION OF MYSELF IN THE ARMS OF PUNK ROCK.

MY CLOSET TURNED AND TURNED AS IT SKEWED THE ACCEPTANCE I WAS FEELING AS A SEXUAL BEING. BECAUSE I KNEW I WAS A WOMAN THE MOMENT I HAD MY FIRST ORGASM TO AN IMAGINARY CAVALCADE OF ORGANS, BODIES, AND ILL-TEMPERED HABITS THAT SUBVERTED MY VERY DEFINITION OF "WOMAN." BUT IT WAS NICE TO ADMINISTER A SOMEWHAT SIMILAR VIBRATION TO MY FAMILY — MY FAMILY WHO HAD NOTHING BUT LOVE FOR ME, HOWEVER DISTANT FROM MY IDENTITY THEIR BLOOD FLOWED.

I GOT HOME AFTER SCHOOL THAT DAY AND STARED AT THE MIRROR FOR A PECULIAR AMOUNT OF TIME. I HAD NOTICED THIS NEW PATTERN FORMULATING OVER THE LAST COUPLE OF MONTHS, WHERE SALVATION FROM ANY FEELINGS OF SELF-DISDAIN COULD ONLY BE BROUGHT FORTH BY GREEN DAY. A GREEN DAY ARTICLE, A TELEVISION APPEARANCE, A DISCUSSION ABOUT GREEN DAY WITH A NEW FRIEND, A SLAP IN THE FACE BY REALITY SAYING TO ME, *"THIS IS NOT YOUR REALITY; IT'S SOMEONE ELSE'S. BUT IT IS YOUR IDENTITY. AND IT CAN BECOME YOUR REALITY IF YOU SOMEHOW CREATE SOMETHING OF YOUR OWN."* AS I RECOILED INTO MY SKIN TO REMEMBER THAT MY REALITY HAD YET TO FORM, I SHED THE SCALING SKIN OF MY ADOLESCENCE AND WATCHED IT TOUGHEN. DURING THE PROCESS, I CONVINCED MYSELF I WAS GOING TO GO INSANE, UNTIL I CAME OUT TO AT LEAST ONE PERSON IN *REAL* LIFE. OR MAYBE UNTIL I LEARNED HOW TO PLAY GUITAR, OR UNTIL I AT LEAST SHARED MY FEELINGS WITH GREEN DAY.

FEELINGS THAT MADE ME FEEL CLAUSTROPHOBIC AND ALONE.

I HAD TALKED TO THE COUNSELOR FOR A MINUTE. COUNSELOR JENKINS. SHE SEEMED TO ALWAYS KNOW WHAT TO SAY, WITHOUT ME EVEN HAVING TO COME OUT OF THE CLOSET TO HER. I TALKED ABOUT PUNK ROCK AS MY IDENTITY, AND I HOPED IT READ AS "GAY" OR "BI" OR "SOMETHING."

SHE REMINDED ME THAT IT'S NATURAL WHEN ONE'S NEW IDENTITY TAKES OVER, AND SHE ECHOED MY CONVICTIONS ABOUT PUNK ROCK IDOLS BEING BETTER THAN RELATIONSHIPS.

MS. JENKINS MADE ALL CRAZY PRE-TEENS SEEM PERFECTLY HEALTHY, ALTHOUGH I COULD STILL ACKNOWLEDGE WHEN I WAS POSSIBLY CROSSING THE LINE I DREW FOR MYSELF.

LIKE, INSPIRE ME TO SHAVE MY HEAD?

WELL, SHAPING YOUR IDENTITY AFTER SOMEONE WHO YOU HAVE A CRUSH ON MAY BE *SLIGHTLY* MORE UNHEALTHY THAN DOING SO AFTER SOMEONE WHO INSPIRES YOU, BUT ALWAYS REMEMBER THAT THE BEST CRUSHES ARE THE ONES WHO ALSO INSPIRE YOU.

COUNSELOR OF THE YEAR AWARD

I WONDERED IF I WAS CREATING THE INABILITY TO FEEL CENTERED ON MY OWN. BY CHOOSING NOT TO COME OUT. BY BEING AFRAID OF CUBAN VALUES AND FEARING MY FAMILY'S REACTION. I WONDERED IF MY INABILITY TO COME OUT TO ANYONE REAL, AS OPPOSED TO THE DISTANT DEITY THAT HAD BECOME MY FAVORITE BAND, WAS COMPLETELY 100% MY FAULT?

I CUT THROUGH MY SELF-DOUBT AS I CUT OUT MY FAVORITE GREEN DAY PHOTOS TO DECORATE THE OUT-SIDE OF MY SCRAP-BOOK, WHICH WOULD SOMEDAY DOCUMENT THEIR ENTIRE EXISTENCE. I WAS STILL ON A DEEP TREK TO FIND THE *ADVOCATE* ARTICLE WHERE BILLIE JOE DISCUSSES HIS OWN SEXU-ALITY, AS WELL AS HIS AND ADRIENNE'S HOPE TO PROVIDE SUPPORT FOR ALL GAY CHILDREN. FOR NOW, I AT LEAST HAD A GOOD INCH-AND-A-HALF OF MAGAZINES AND CLIPPINGS.

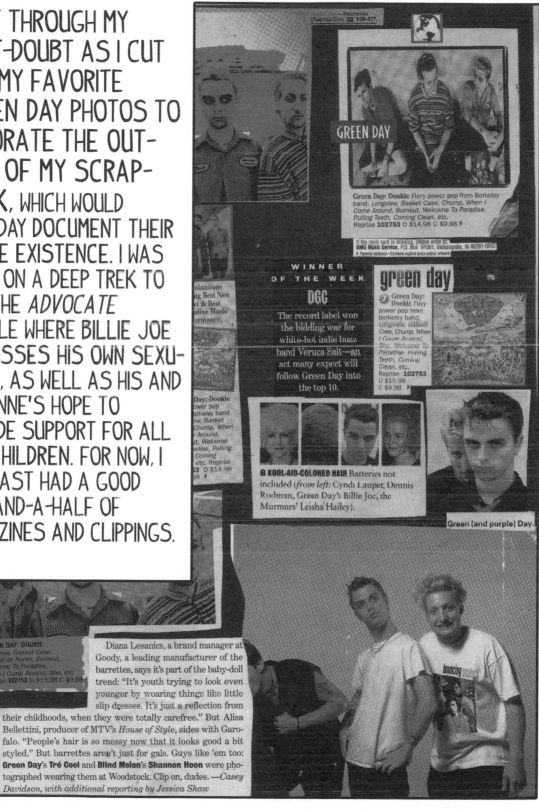

—Insomniac
(Reprise/Sire) 138-477

GREEN DAY

Green Day: Dookie Fiery power pop from Berkeley band. *Longview, Basket Case, Chump, When I Come Around, Burnout, Welcome To Paradise, Pulling Teeth, Coming Clean,* etc.
Reprise **102753** D $14.98 C $9.98

If the reply card is missing, please write to:
BMG Music Service, P.O. Box 91001, Indianapolis, IN 46291-0002
♪ Parental Advisory—Contains explicit lyrics and/or artwork.

WINNER
OF THE WEEK
DGC
The record label won the bidding war for white-hot indie buzz band Veruca Salt—an act many expect will follow Green Day into the top 10.

green day
Green Day: Dookie Fiery power pop from Berkeley band. *Longview, Basket Case, Chump, When I Come Around, She, Welcome To Paradise, Pulling Teeth, Coming Clean,* etc.
Reprise **102753** D $15.98 C $9.98 ♪

8 KOOL-AID-COLORED HAIR Batteries not included (*from left:* Cyndi Lauper, Dennis Rodman, Green Day's Billie Joe, the Murmurs' Leisha Hailey).

Green (and purple) Day.

GREEN DAY: DOOKIE
Longview, Basket Case, Sassafras Roots, Burnout, Welcome To Paradise, When I Come Around, She, etc.
Reprise 102753 D $15.98 C $9.98

Diana Lesanics, a brand manager at Goody, a leading manufacturer of the barrettes, says it's part of the baby-doll trend: "It's youth trying to look even younger by wearing things like little slip dresses. It's just a reflection from their childhoods, when they were totally carefree." But Alisa Bellettini, producer of MTV's *House of Style,* sides with Garofalo. "People's hair is so messy now that it looks good a bit styled." But barrettes aren't just for gals. Guys like 'em too: **Green Day's Tré Cool** and **Blind Melon's Shannon Hoon** were photographed wearing them at Woodstock. Clip on, dudes. —*Casey Davidson, with additional reporting by Jessica Shaw*

I WAS ALWAYS LOOKING BOTH WAYS BEFORE I OPENED MY MOUTH. WAS I A COWARD WITH NO BALLS, OR WERE SOCIETY, CULTURE, AND EXPERIENCE TRULY INHIBITING MY GOALS TO COME OUT BECAUSE I'M A GIRL, AND I HAD TO JUSTIFY THE FEMALE-BODIED MANIFESTATION OF MY OWN BALLS?

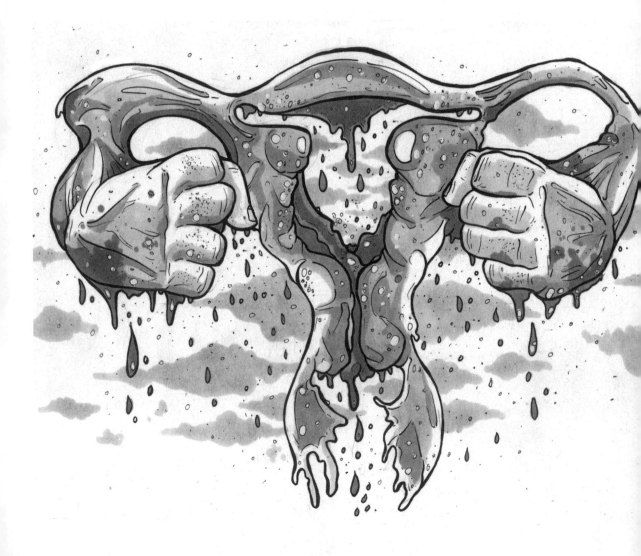

USED TO CRAWL INTO BED AT THE END OF THE DAY, AND REST ASSURED THAT AS MUCH AS IT WAS ME BEING AFRAID AND BEING FOURTEEN, I WAS AFRAID FOR A REASON. I WAS PERPETUALLY DISMISSED AS A HUMAN AND BY THE UNSPOKEN LAWS OF CASUAL HOMOPHOBIA, NO MATTER HOW AGGRESSIVE I COULD BE WHEN I WAS GIVEN THE SPACE TO BE MYSELF, OR AT LEAST, HAIL GREEN DAY.

WAS SHACKLED TO TRADITION, SO I TRIED TO REBUILD BASED ON THE ASSUMED RESULTS OF WHAT MAY HAVE BEEN IMAGINARY CONVERSATIONS BETWEEN CELIA CRUZ AND WENDY O. WILLIAMS IN A BISTRO IN HIALEAH.

MY PERIOD SEARED, AS DID MY ANXIETY. THIS WAS MY REALITY, AND IF YOU CAN'T BEAT 'EM, YOU JOIN 'EM, BUT IT WAS SAD . . .

UUGGHH!

I DON'T WANT TO **OBJECTIFY** YOU!!!!!!

. . . THAT GUSHING ABOUT A CRUSH ON A MAN IN ORDE TO FEEL ACCEPTED BY SOCIETY WAS SLIGHTLY EASIER THAN BEING AGGRESSIVELY REPRESSED WIT SO MUCH TO HID

I WALKED AROUND MY ROOM PACING BETWEEN MISERY AND ECSTASY, TRYING TO UNDERSTAND THAT GENDER IS FLUID LIKE ATTRACTION. FLASHES OF ALEX, SABRINA, MY FAVORITE NEW CELEBRITY ELLEN DEGENERES FROM THE SHOW *THESE FRIENDS OF MINE* AND "THE TRUTH" GRABBED MY WRISTS AND SLAPPED THEM AFFECTIONATELY.

I DID NOT WANT TO PRETEND TO BE STRAIGHT FOR ANYONE. I DID NOT WANT TO PRETEND THAT GREEN DAY WAS NOT THE CATALYST FOR MY SELF-ACCEPTANCE, BUT I ALSO DID NOT WANT TO BELIEVE THAT GREEN DAY WAS MY ONLY BEACON OF LIGHT. I WANTED TO BELIEVE IN THE PROSPECT OF MY FRIENDSHIPS AND THE PROSPECT OF MY COMING OUT, BUT I WAS STARTING TO REALIZE A LONG JOURNEY STOOD IN THE WAY. I WENT TO SLEEP AND HOPED FOR THE DAY AFTER TO BE BETTER, OR AT LEAST FOR MY PERIOD TO *STOP*.

CHAPTER SIX

I DECLARE I DON'T CARE
NO MORE

IT WAS TIME FOR THAT DREAM AGAIN. THE ONE WHERE I GREW UP, CAME OUT, AND WENT OUT — WITH ALEX — TO THE GREEN DAY SHOW. TOGETHER WE SWAYED ALONG TO THE TUNES THAT JUSTIFIED OUR SELF-WORTH, OR MINE, SINCE, BASED ON ALEX'S T-SHIRTS, KMFDM SEEMED TO TAKE THE HERO CAKE. BUT THIS WAS MY DREAM, GODDAMMIT.

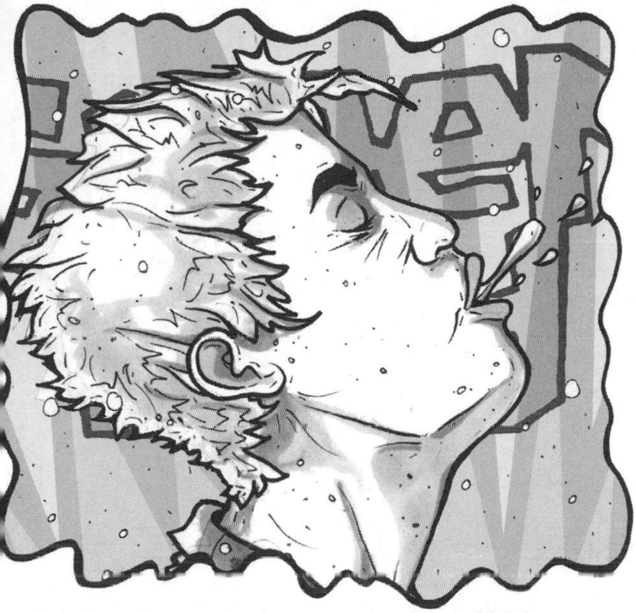

BILLIE JOE HAWKED A GENTLE LUGIE INTO
THE AIR WHILE GRAVITY DEFIED TIME AND SPACE.

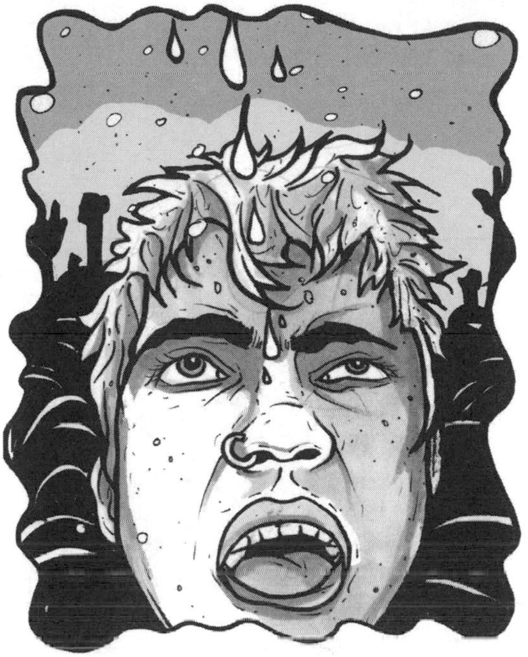

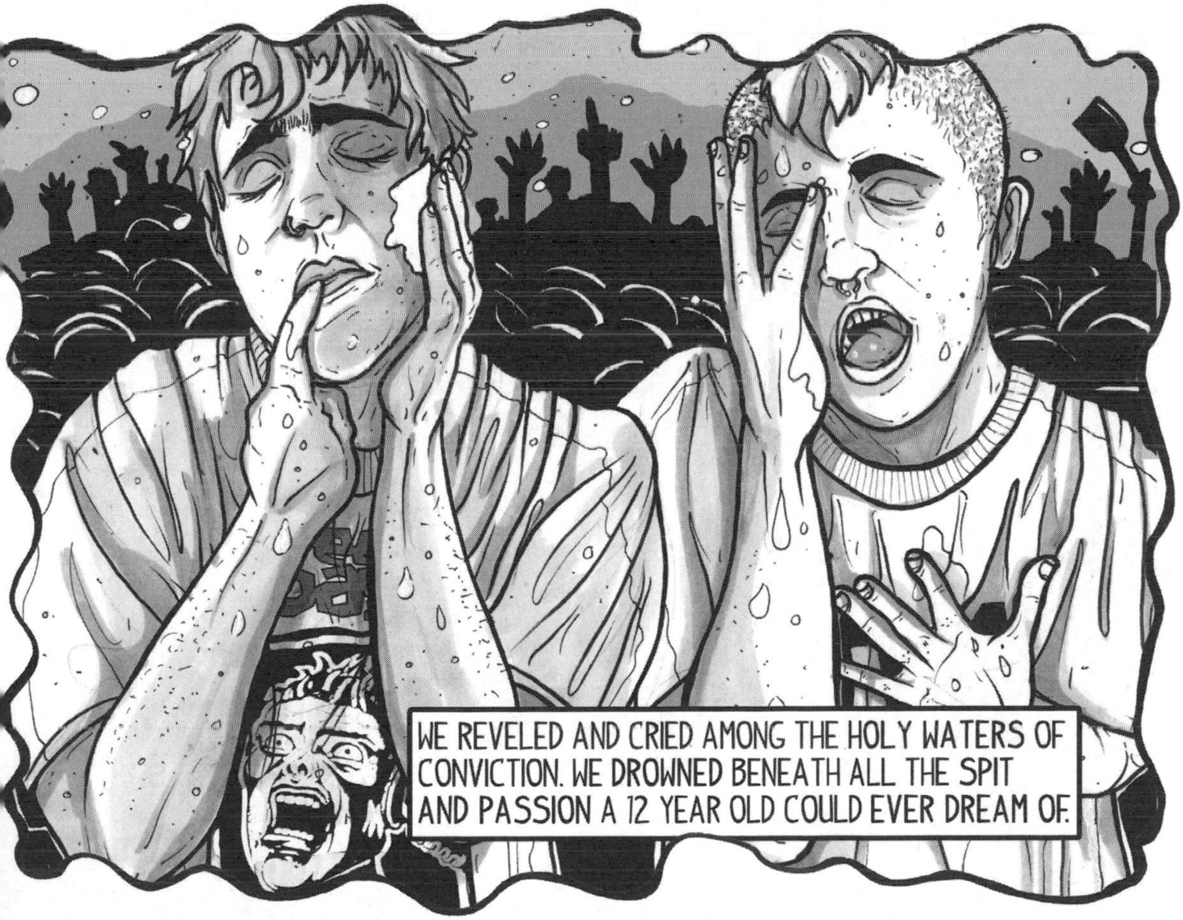
WE REVELED AND CRIED AMONG THE HOLY WATERS OF CONVICTION. WE DROWNED BENEATH ALL THE SPIT AND PASSION A 12 YEAR OLD COULD EVER DREAM OF.

THEN WE ALL WENT **TO THE INTERNATIONAL MALL** TO EAT **BURGER KING.**

THEN I WOKE UP. MY PERIOD ENDED, AND I HAD TO GET TO SCHOOL. BUT ALL I WANTED TO DO WAS REPLAY THE LAST 8 HOURS IN MY HEAD, OVER AND OVER.

I HAD TO SIT IN THE OFFICE BEFORE CLASS IN ORDER TO GET AN EXCUSE NOTICE FOR MISSING SCHOOL. I WAS FORCED INTO LISTENING TO AN EYE-OPENING DISCUSSION BETWEEN ALUMNI OFFICE CLERKS.

BUT **HOMOSEXUALITY IS A DISEASE!** I DON'T THINK PEOPLE SHOULD BE PUNISHED FOR BEING SICK, *YOU KNOW?*

AY, BUT IT'S JUST SO *WEIRD.*

YEAH, *IT IS . . . HEH HEH . . .*

HEH HEH HEH . . .

AY, BUT POBRESITO, YOU KNOW? I FEEL BAD FOR THE ABUSE THEY GET.

YEAH, NOBODY DESERVES **ABUSE,** BUT AY, I DON'T KNOW, **HOW COME NOBODY HAD THIS** *DISEASE* WHEN WE WERE KIDS, *YOU KNOW?*

BUENO . . . *ITS THE 90s!*

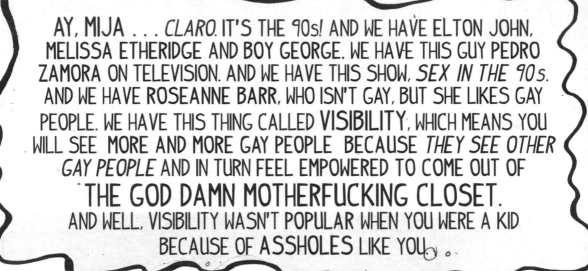

AY, MIJA . . . *CLARO*. IT'S THE 90s! AND WE HAVE ELTON JOHN, MELISSA ETHERIDGE AND BOY GEORGE. WE HAVE THIS GUY PEDRO ZAMORA ON TELEVISION. AND WE HAVE THIS SHOW, *SEX IN THE 90s*. AND WE HAVE ROSEANNE BARR, WHO ISN'T GAY, BUT SHE LIKES GAY PEOPLE. WE HAVE THIS THING CALLED **VISIBILITY**, WHICH MEANS YOU WILL SEE MORE AND MORE GAY PEOPLE BECAUSE *THEY SEE OTHER GAY PEOPLE* AND IN TURN FEEL EMPOWERED TO COME OUT OF **THE GOD DAMN MOTHERFUCKING CLOSET.** AND WELL, VISIBILITY WASN'T POPULAR WHEN YOU WERE A KID BECAUSE OF **ASSHOLES** LIKE YOU.

I OFFICIALLY FEARED THE REST OF MY DAY.

MARIMAR HAD A FEW POPULAR FRIENDS — JESSICA AND YELI. I GREW ATTACHED TO MARIMAR, BUT I FELT UNWELL AROUND HER FRIENDS.

ON A PLAIN OLD TUESDAY, JESSICA, YELI, AND MARIMAR INFORMED ME THAT THEY HAD THE NEW *SEVEN-TEEN* MAGAZINE IN THEIR POSSESSION, WHICH HAD A PHOTO OF GREEN DAY INSIDE OF IT. BILLIE JOE HAD APPARENTLY WON SOME SORT OF *CUTE BOY CONTEST?* GRANTED, I DID NOT WANT TO BE CAUGHT DEAD WITH THAT SORT OF THING ON ME, BUT I WANTED THE PHOTOS BAD. THEY ASKED ME TO MEET THEM AFTER SCHOOL SO THEY COULD GIVE ME THE MAGAZINE, OR AT LEAST THE PAGE WITH GREEN DAY ON IT.

DURING THE LAST CLASS OF THE DAY, I GAZED UP AT THE CLOCK EVERY 2-3 SECONDS. IT FELT AS IF THE HOUR HAND WAS ABOUT TO DO CARTWHEELS AND DECLARE THE END OF INERTIA.

INSTEAD THE SECOND HAND KEPT TICKING AND TOCKING, SLOWER AND SLOWER. AS I WATCHED, I PICKED MY EARS. AS MY EARS BLED, I SUNK INTO MY CHAIR AND PUT ON MY HEADPHONES. THE DAY WOULD *NEVER* BE OVER, I THOUGHT.

FINALLY, CLASS WAS OVER, AND I HEADED OVER TO MARIMAR AND HER FRIENDS.

MARIMAR TORE UP THE INTERIOR OF THE MAGAZINE, MAKING SURE TO GET ALL OF THE GREEN DAY CONTENT.

EVERYONE LAUGHED. I CRINGED AND FELT A RARE BLEND OF DESPAIR, HEARTACHE, AND ALOOFNESS. PART OF ME BELIEVED I WAS ABOVE THIS — ME AND GREEN DAY LAY EXALTED IN THAT ALTERNATE PLANE WHERE MY INHIBITIONS, INSECURITIES, AND SELF SPRAWLED MINDLESSLY, BUT JOYFULLY. PART OF ME FELT STUPID AND TERRIBLE, OBVIOUSLY UNDESERVING OF SUBSTANTIAL FRIENDSHIPS BECAUSE HERE I WAS, WITH A PERFECTLY GOOD FRIEND, BUT FOR *SOME* REASON I DESERVED PUBLIC RIDICULE. I GUESS I WAS CRAZY.

I WISHED I COULD HAVE SCREAMED IT OUT LOUD, BUT I DIDN'T HAVE IT IN ME. THE TORN SHEETS OF *SEVENTEEN* MAGAZINE WERE SPREAD OUT ON THE GROUND. BILLIE JOE'S EAR RESTED ON ONE END OF THE FLOOR, AND MIKE DIRNT'S ON THE OTHER. CRUMBLED-UP TEXT AND A SUGGESTION OF TRE COOL'S FACE LANDED BESIDE MY SHOE. I STEPPED ON IT AND LOOKED DOWN AND WANTED TO IMMEDIATELY FORGET ANYTHING HAD EVER HAPPENED.

BUT I COULDN'T, BECAUSE I WAS A GEMINI, AMONG OTHER DEBILITATING LIFE CIRCUMSTANCES.

I GUESS I JUST STOPPED TALKING TO MARIMAR. FROM THAT POINT ON, OUR CONNECTION BECAME UNRESOLVED. BUT WE TALKED ENOUGH TO REACH A BETTER PLACE WHERE WE KNEW, DEEP INSIDE, THAT THE SAME OLD FRIENDSHIP WOULD RISE ABOVE THE ASHES OF THAT DAY.

SUDDENLY LOSING FRIENDS BROUGHT A NEW LEVEL OF ALIENATION. I DIDN'T KNOW WHAT I WAS DOING EXACTLY; JUST KNEW THAT EVERY TIME I WOULD GATHER CONFIDENCE AND EMBRACE A LEVEL OF SELF-RIGHTEOUSNESS THAT HELPED ME LOVE MYSELF A LITTLE BIT MORE MY ANGER WOULD SHOW. I WONDERED IF THE DISTRESSED VERSION OF ME DID SOMETHING WRONG, SOMETHING BESIDES CHALLENGE THE STATUS QUO BECAUSE I WAS BORN INTO AN IDENTITY THAT LEFT ME DRAINED.

SURROUNDED BY MY THINGS, I FELT LIKE I WAS DROWNING IN THE BACK CORNER OF MY CLOSET — THE DAMPEST CLOSET IN THE HOUSE. THE ONE THAT HAD BEEN PINCHED BY A HURRICANE AND CLUTTERED BY DISCARDED ITEMS. THE ONE EVERYONE HAD FORGOTTEN ABOUT.

I CRAWLED INSIDE AND WROTE UNTIL I JUSTIFIED MY PAIN. I WROTE ENOUGH TO MAKE SENSE OF MYSELF AND TO FEEL AS IF I WAS DOING *SOMETHING* WITH MY INSANITY -- SOMETHING PRODUCTIVE AND USEFUL, FOR THE FUTURE, LIKE MATERIAL FOR POP-PUNK SONG LYRICS. I WROTE TERRIBLE THINGS ABOUT MARIMAR AND HER FRIENDS, AND I WROTE TERRIBLE THINGS ABOUT MYSELF, IN AN ATTEMPT TO MAKE ALL OF US LOOK BAD ENOUGH THAT NOBODY WAS AT FAULT, BESIDES HUMAN SOCIALIZATION . . . IT'S WHAT MS. JENKINS WOULD HAVE MADE ME FEEL. SHE ALWAYS ASKED US TO REMEMBER THAT AT THE END OF THE DAY, WE ALWAYS HAD OURSELVES. GRANTED, I WOULD ONLY GO TO HER OFFICE WITH THE MERE GOAL OF RUNNING INTO ALEX, BUT LITTLE BY LITTLE, I BELIEVED IN MS. JENKINS. SHE ALWAYS FOUND A WAY TO MAKE EVERYONE SEEM RIGHT, WHETHER OR NOT THEY DID WRONG.

I GUESS THAT'S WHAT SHE WAS THERE FOR. SO ALL THE KIDS COULD STOP BLINDLY TREATING EACH OTHER LIKE SHIT.

"DO YOU EVER THINK BACK? TO ANOTHER TIME? DOES IT BRING YOU SO DOWN THAT YOU THOUGHT YOU LOST YOUR MIND?"

"DO YOU EVER WANT TO LEAD A LONG TRAIL OF DESTRUCTION? AND MOW DOWN ALL THE BULLSHIT THAT CONFRONTS YOU?"

"DO YOU EVER BUILD UP ALL THE SMALL THINGS IN YOUR HEAD AND MAKE ONE PROBLEM THAT ADDS UP TO NOTHING?"

I EVENTUALLY SURVIVED. AND I WAS ALMOST 13. MAYBE I CAN BLAME GREEN DAY? MAYBE I WASN'T MEANT TO TOTALLY SELF-DESTRUCT JUST YET, BUT MILDLY SELF-DESTRUCT, LITTLE BY LITTLE, SO I COULD REHABILITATE MYSELF LITTLE BY LITTLE? NONETHELESS, I HAD FOUND A RELATIVELY SOUND BALANCE BETWEEN NORMALCY AND INSANITY.

WHEN I WAS ALONE, I WAS SELF-ASSURED. I WAS GAY. GAY GAY GAY. I WOULD SAY THIS TO MYSELF, IN AN ASYLUM CREATED BY THE VIBRATIONS IN MY HEADPHONES AND THE VIABLE DETERMINATION THAT LIFE COULD EXIST WHILE HARSH RESENTMENT EXISTED OUTSIDE OF IT, STILL AFFECTING IT, BUT NEVER ENOUGH TO STOP IT. LIFE'S BASIC OBSTACLES, LIKE SELF-HATE AND AN UNSUPPORTED SEXUALITY, WERE LIKE HOMEWORK. THEY ARE GOING TO BE THERE WHETHER YOU LIKE IT OR NOT; BUT YOU *DON'T* HAVE TO DEAL WITH IT IF YOU ARE NOT PREPARED. AND IF ONE OR TWO THINGS IN MY LIFE HAD TO FUNCTION ON DIFFERENT LEVELS, THEN I GUESS I WAS OKAY, AS LONG AS THEY COULD FUNCTION.

AY *CRISTINITA*, SOPLA LAS VELAS OTRA VEZ PARA ESTA PHOTO!

AY, *CRISTINITA* PORQUE TE ENSERASTE EN EL CUARTO!?

MAYBE I COULD BE IN THE CLOSET UNTIL I WAS READY TO COME OUT? THE CLOSET COULD MANIFEST INTO A SANCTUARY, FOR THE SAKE OF UPROOTING THE THINGS I THOUGHT I LOST, LIKE MY ETHNICITY, MY CHILDHOOD, AND MY GIVEN SOUL. I COULD REINVENT THEM. TREASURE THEM IN RETROSPECT BUT SMASH THEIR UNFORTUNATE IDIOSYNCRASIES WHEN NECESSARY. TRANSFORMING TRADITIONAL VALUES INTO RADICAL IDEAS WAS JUST PLAIN DIFFICULT, BECAUSE SALVAGING MY CULTURE FELT AS IMPORTANT AS MAINTAINING MYSELF.

I WAS CURRENTLY IN A REMOVED PLANE OF LIFE WHERE CLARITA AND I SAT AROUND WITH OUR TAPES, CDs, AND OUR HAPHAZARD ASPIRATIONS. THAT SUMMER, WE TALKED ON THE PHONE FOR HOURS ABOUT PUNK, METAL, WOMEN WE FOUND ATTRACTIVE WHILE NOT SPECIFICALLY COMING OUT, MEN WE FOUND ATTRACTIVE WHILE NOT SPECIFICALLY BEING STRAIGHT, AND THE BLANK STARES SOCIETY GAVE US DESPITE HOW MUCH WE HAD MOLDED OURSELVES TO THEIR EXPECTATIONS OF LIFE AND GENDER. WE TALKED ABOUT OURSELVES AND HOW EXCITED WE WERE FOR THE EIGHTH GRADE WHEN I WOULD FINALLY BE ALLOWED TO GET A HAIRCUT. FROM THIS SANCTUARY WE CALLED A FRACTION OF HOME, WE BUILT OURSELVES AN IDENTITY. WE EVADED BACKLASH TO THE CULTURE WE LOVED, BUT HELD ON TO THE INEVITABLY INTERNAL *(AND QUESTIONABLY ETERNAL)* BATTLE WITH THE PARTS OF CULTURE WE COULD NOT SUPPORT, SYMPATHIZE WITH, PRETEND TO LISTEN TO, PRETEND TO UNDERSTAND, OR PRETEND TO RESPECT.

CLARITA SEEMED SO SERENE, SO OKAY WITH THE FACT THAT LIFE WAS UNCERTAIN AND THAT SOMETIMES WE ARE BOUND TO FEEL UNSUPPORTED. IT WAS THAT CAPRICORN NATURE THAT EXPLAINED HER UNFATHOMABLE ABILITY TO JUST *DEAL*. AS A GEMINI, I ALWAYS WANTED TO KNOW WHAT WAS GOING TO HAPPEN IF I DID SOMETHING THIS WAY OR THAT WAY, AND I WANTED EVERYONE ELSE TO KNOW AS WELL. WHEN IN THE END, I JUST NEEDED CLARITA TO REMIND ME THAT IT WASN'T MY JOB TO ACT UPON OR UNDERSTAND ANYTHING, UNLESS I TRULY FELT LIKE I COULDN'T LIVE WITHOUT IT.

I DECIDED THAT FOR NOW I COULD LIVE WITHOUT MY CULTURE FULLY UNDERSTANDING MY SEXUAL ORIENTATION. FOR NOW, IT WAS EASIER TO UNDERSTAND MY FAMILY'S TIES TO TRADITIONAL VALUES AS I SLOWLY UNVEILED MY UNTRADITIONAL EXISTENCE, IN ORDER TO EVENTUALLY LET GO, ONCE I WAS READY. I REALIZED I HAD TO GET TO KNOW MYSELF INTERNALLY NOW THAT I HAD REALIZED WHO I WAS. I NEEDED TO GET TO KNOW MY CHOSEN SELF, THE SELF THAT CHOSE ME.

BASICALLY, I NEEDED TO ORDER THE GAYEST, MOST POLITICAL ITEMS ON THE LOOKOUT RECORDS CATALOG, WITH THE MONEY I GOT FOR MY BIRTHDAY.

I TRIED TO DISASSOCIATE MY FAMILY FROM THE EVIL VALUES THEY WERE BORN INTO, THE VALUES THAT I BELIEVED HUMANITY WOULD EVENTUALLY REJECT. FRANKLY, I DID NOT KNOW HOW OR WHEN THIS WOULD HAPPEN, BUT I KNEW ONE THING: I WANTED TO BE *CUBANA* AS MUCH AS I WANTED TO BE *GAY*. TRADITIONAL WAYS OF THINKING WERE GONNA HAPPEN, BUT I DIDN'T WANT TO LOSE WHAT I OTHERWISE TOOK PRIDE IN.

I DIDN'T LIKE **AMERICA** AND THE THINGS THAT I FELT CHALLENGED THE CREATIVE PURITY OF MY **CULTURE**. I WAS POLLO FRICASE, LA VAQUITA, Y LA FASTIDIOSA. LA QUE NO SE PARECE A LAS OTRAS CHIQUITAS, **PERO LA HERMOSA** — BECAUSE I TRIED TO BE THE BEST I COULD, **EVEN IF IT SCARED THE OTHER GIRLS AT SCHOOL.**

DEEP INSIDE, I WAS BURNING. I WANTED PEOPLE TO STOP COMPLAINING AND TO STOP HOPING FOR PLANETARY HOMOGENIZATION. SO I ATTEMPTED A CONSTANT STATE OF MEDITATION, IN ORDER TO MAINTAIN SOME SORT OF CONNECTION TO CULTURE WITHOUT DEFEAT, BECAUSE I WAS NOT *A CERTAIN WAY* AND I HAD TO DO WHAT I COULD TO SURVIVE. I WANTED TO BREATHE. I WANTED TO THINK IN SPANISH, BATHE IN MOJO CRIOLLO, DREAM IN CUBA, AND SATURATE IN MY CLOSET.

I WANTED TO SIMMER AND SEAR ON THE 90-DEGREE PAVEMENT, ON A STROLL DOWN CORAL WAY, INHALING 10 CORQUETTAS DE JAMON AND A *MONTES DE OCA PIZZA CUBANA*, HOLDING ONTO SOMEONE'S HAND, AND HOLDING ONTO MYSELF.

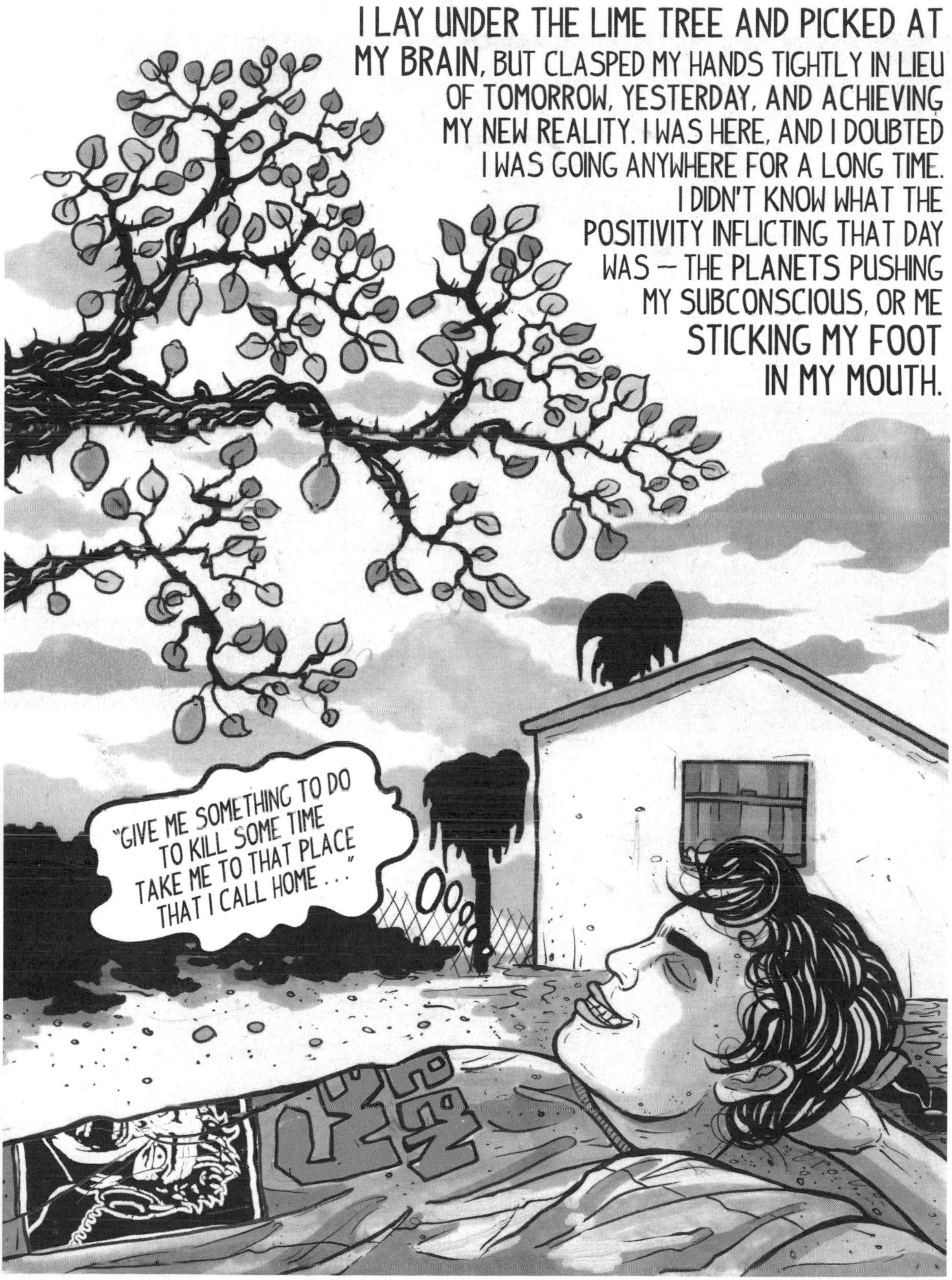
I LAY UNDER THE LIME TREE AND PICKED AT MY BRAIN, BUT CLASPED MY HANDS TIGHTLY IN LIEU OF TOMORROW, YESTERDAY, AND ACHIEVING MY NEW REALITY. I WAS HERE, AND I DOUBTED I WAS GOING ANYWHERE FOR A LONG TIME. I DIDN'T KNOW WHAT THE POSITIVITY INFLICTING THAT DAY WAS — THE PLANETS PUSHING MY SUBCONSCIOUS, OR ME STICKING MY FOOT IN MY MOUTH.
"GIVE ME SOMETHING TO DO TO KILL SOME TIME TAKE ME TO THAT PLACE THAT I CALL HOME . . ."

IT WAS AROUND 4 P.M. AND MAMA CALLED ME TO COME BACK INTO THE HOUSE BECAUSE LUNCH WAS BEING SERVED. MY FAMILY BUILT A SHEATH ABOVE MY HEAD THAT PROTECTED ME FROM HURRICANES AND SELF-HATE. MAMA AND YEYA WOULD CHOP VEGETABLES, STEW MEATS, AWAKEN FLAVORS, AND HONOR THE SPICE THAT STREAMED THROUGH OUR BLOOD VESSELS. WHEN LUNCH WAS READY, FIFI AND I FACED UN PLATO DE ROPA VIEJA, PAPAS SARCOCHADA, WHITE RICE, AND BATIDOS DE MAMEY ON FOLDABLE TV TRAYS. WE COULD LAUGH AND RESURRECT OUR 13 YEARS OF CHILDHOOD THAT WOULD NEVER FULLY GO AWAY.

... THROUGH EVERY STRAY GAY SLUR MANEUVERING ITS WAY THROUGH MY FAMILY'S DIALOGUE AND EXITING THE LOOSE MOUTHS OF YOUNG, FIERY, SARCASTIC KIDS, I PUT SOCIALIZATION ON THAT CURB AGAIN. I WOULD PUT IT THERE BEFORE EVERY LUNCH, EVERY DINNER, EVERY LAUGH, EVERY CHRISTMAS, EVERY BIRTH-DAY, AND BEFORE EVERY RECONNECTION.

I LIKED TO SEE MY CLOSET AS A SAFE AND ALTERNATE UNIVERSE OF US VS. THEM, AND NOW VS. LATER. IN MY CLOSET, THE OCEANS AND CREATURES WOULD COALESCE IN SUPPORT OF MY IDENTITY.

SOMETIMES THE DOORWAYS FELT LIKE PILLARS, THE CLOTHING ON THE RACKS LIKE TROPICAL FOLIAGE, AND THE GROUND LIKE THE OCEAN. I RODE THE CURRENTS WITH MY CONSCIOUS MIND AND I LEARNED TO TUCK THAT MIND AWAY IF I NEEDED TO, ALTHOUGH I KNEW I NEVER WANTED TO. I LEARNED TO NOT ATTACK MYSELF FOR THIS, AS I DEVELOPED A NEW SENSE OF STRENGTH IN THE OASIS I HAD CREATED.

I LIKED TO WATCH THE SUNSET AS IF IT WAS THE LAST DAY ON EARTH. I WOULD INSPECT EVERY ABYSS OF NEON-PINK LIGHT BECAUSE I KNEW THAT TOMMOROW MIGHT NOT LOOK LIKE THIS. I WOULD SIT THERE AND WAIT FOR THE SKY TO TURN MY FAVORITE SHADE OF SATURATED PERIWINKLE, AND I WOULD WATCH UNTIL IT WENT AWAY.

I SLEPT WITH A NIGHT LIGHT ON. I THOUGHT THE DARKNESS WAS JUST PLAIN FRIGHTENING — BUT IT SEEMED TO MAKE ABSOLUTE SENSE WHEN THERE WAS JUST THE RIGHT AMOUNT OF LIGHT.

THANK YOU TO EVERYONE WHO PARTICIPATED IN THE PROCESS OF CREATING THIS NOVEL, WHETHER IT WAS **POSING AS A CHARACTER,** MAKING ME DINNER WHEN ALL I COULD DO WAS DRAW, MORAL SUPPORT, OR CONSTRUCTIVE CRITICISM.

THANK YOU TO EVERYONE AND EVERYTHING WHO MADE THIS NOVEL POSSIBLE: MY BLOOD FAMILY, MY QUEER FAMILY, GREEN DAY, FLORIDA, NYC, THE SF BAY, BROOKLYN QUEER PUNKS, THE HOMEWRECKERS, SANDY AND THE RATS, SISTER SPIT, SUPPORT NY, PHILLY'S PISSED, THE FEMINIST PRESS, THE DEPARTMENT OF TRANSFORMATION, THE FEMMES OF COLOR BRUNCH, LOOKOUT RECORDS, ADELINE RECORDS, RIOT GRRRL, CELIA CRUZ, ROSEANNE BARR, AND QUEER TRAILBLAZERS.

fp

PUBLISHED IN 2012 BY THE FEMINIST PRESS
AT THE CITY UNIVERSITY OF NEW YORK
THE GRADUATE CENTER
365 FIFTH AVENUE, SUITE 5406
NEW YORK, NY 10016

FEMINISTPRESS.ORG

FIRST PRINTING NOVEMBER 2012

LIBRARY OF CONGRESS CATALOGING-IN-PUBLICATION DATA
ROAD, CRISTY C.
  SPIT AND PASSION / CRISTY C. ROAD.
     P. CM.
  ISBN 978-1-55861-807-7
  1. ROAD, CRISTY C. — COMIC BOOKS, STRIPS, ETC. 2. COMING OUT (SEXUAL
ORIENTATION) — COMIC BOOKS, STRIPS, ETC. 3. GREEN DAY (MUSICAL GROUP) —
COMIC BOOKS, STRIPS, ETC. 4. GRAPHIC NOVELS. I. TITLE.
  PN6727.R555B33 2008
  741.5'973 — DC23
  [B]